What every hostess needs to know

CYNTHIA PAYNE

# ENTERTAINING AT HOME

— ▫ —

*101 Party Hints from
Britain's Most Popular
Hostess*

PENGUIN BOOKS

Penguin Books Ltd, 27 Wrights Lane, London W8 5TZ (Publishing and Editorial)
*and* Harmondsworth, Middlesex, England (Distribution and Warehouse)
Viking Penguin Inc., 40 West 23rd Street, New York, New York 10010, USA
Penguin Books Australia Ltd, Ringwood, Victoria, Australia
Penguin Books Canada Ltd, 2801 John Street, Markham, Ontario, Canada L3R 1B4
Penguin Books (NZ) Ltd, 182–190 Wairau Road, Auckland 10, New Zealand

First published 1987
Reprinted 1987

Edited by Terence Blacker

Designed by Shape of Things, London EC1

Filmset in Garamond Simoncini
by The Creative Text Partnership

Printed and bound in Great Britain by
William Clowes Limited, Beccles and London

WITH SPECIAL THANKS TO GLORIA WALKER
FOR HER HELP AND SUPPORT

# CONTENTS

# INTRODUCTION
## WHAT EVERY HOSTESS NEEDS TO KNOW

SOME people are born entertainers. Some entertain only after years of practice. Some have entertaining thrust upon them. I belong to the last category. Party-giving, like so many of the best things in my life, has been thrust upon me.

The fact is that the best fun I've ever had has always been in company, entertaining people. Of course, these days I'm not able to have the kind of upstairs-downstairs party I've enjoyed in the past without half the Vice Squad breaking my front door down, but somehow, somewhere, I'll be entertaining all the same. It's in the blood.

This book contains everything a hostess needs to know about home entertainment Cynthia Payne style – with the laughs and without the hassles. But, before you send out the first invitation, order the wine or book the live striptease act, you should ask yourself these all-important questions.

———————— □ ————————

WHY GIVE A PARTY? • You need to *want* to give a party – it shouldn't be a duty or a shortcut to popularity or some sort of service to the community. Entertaining at home should be a treat for yourself, before anyone else.

It helps if you're gregarious in the first place. I've always liked to have a lot of people around me – as a little girl, I used to go about with a gang of boys. I started holding parties

My first party, held at the Victoria flat in 1956.

regularly more out of loneliness than anything else. I was working very hard day after day running a brothel in Great Portland Street and, although I made friends with the girls and many of the men, it was quite a solitary sort of life. Men would come to the flat, I'd chat to them in the kitchen if they had to wait, sometimes I'd give them a cup of tea afterwards, but it was never like a real party. And naturally, I could hardly go around telling people what I did.

Away from the brothel, I was living in a flat with a couple of old friends of mine, Ron and Jim. We all enjoyed a laugh and we used to have friends round quite often. It seemed natural to start giving parties on a regular basis.

My very first party was in 1957, when I was still working as a waitress. We had got the drink and the food in and were all ready to enjoy ourselves when we discovered that there was one thing missing – guests. Ron and Jim went down to the Two Eyes, a famous beatnik hangout in Soho where Tommy Steele used to sing. 'There's a party on in Victoria,' they'd say. 'Lots of food and drink. Everyone's welcome.'

That solved the problem. Loads of beatniks came back to the house and the place was soon rocking.

There were a few odd characters there that night, I remember. One was a man called Ironfoot Jack, whom I later discovered was well known in the West End. He wore a long cloak and a cavalier's hat and, of course, he had an iron foot. I was to see a lot odder sights in my career as a hostess, but he seemed pretty exotic at the time.

———————— □ ————————

WHAT SORT OF PARTY SHOULD I GIVE? • Always remember this simple fact: at any decent party, most of the guests have sex on the mind. Food, drink and conversation are fine, but they are rarely, if ever, top of the average partygoer's list of priorities. I soon discovered that if my guests had sex at one of my parties they were happy and relaxed: the evening was a success. In fact, even at that first party, with Ironfoot Jack and

Money was expended upon her footmen Chariots. Musicians Singers. Players dancers. parasites, pimps & Bands. — But in the end the Money of the People — *vide Cobbs. 2. Rev.*

his beatniks, couples were pairing off and disappearing into the bedrooms. I hadn't encouraged it, yet somehow it just happened.

Another advantage of the sex party over more conventional entertainments is that you tend to get a better class of guest. Over the years, I've come to the conclusion that people who are interested in sex tend to be very interesting themselves, in or out of the bedroom.

So, if you want to give the very best entertainment where everyone leaves thinking, 'Now *that* was a party!', then sex must be on the menu.

———— □ ————

## SHOULD I HOLD MY PARTIES AT HOME? • Now that I've
been forced to give up holding sex parties at Ambleside Avenue, I'm often asked: 'Why don't you arrange parties in other people's homes? You could have your party and charge the hosts a fair old whack at the same time.'

That, for me, would defeat the whole object of a party. For people to enjoy themselves, to relax, they need to feel at home – and so do I.

If you don't have the confidence to throw your sort of party in your own house, then you probably shouldn't be holding one in the first place.

———— □ ————

## WILL MY PARTIES BE FOR PLEASURE OR PROFIT? •
For years, I used to give sex parties just for the enjoyment of it, the companionship. I put an ad in a contact magazine, 'KINKY PEOPLE WANTED FOR KINKY PARTIES', and soon

> IN THOSE BOOKS WRITTEN ON THE SUBJECT OF
> ETIQUETTE WHEN OUR MOTHERS WERE YOUNG,
> NO SPACE WAS ALLOTTED TO THE BUSINESS GIRL.
> Della Thompson Lutes, *The Gracious Hostess*, 1923

I was holding little gatherings at regular intervals.

In a way, those were the best parties I ever had. We used to have three girls as guests and they were all so enthusiastic that, more often than not, all the men left having gone upstairs at some point. Looking back on it, the blokes who came to those parties must have thought it was Christmas all year round – free booze, free food, and a group of girls crying out for sex.

In 1970, I started charging for the parties. It made sense from every point of view: I stopped losing money on food and drink and made a small profit, while the men could be guaranteed at least one trip upstairs. The parties got bigger and more lavish. There would be twenty-five or thirty men and perhaps twelve women. Yet, even before I stopped charging following the 1978 raid, the money was never that important to me. It was the excitement, the laughs, and, of course, the idea that we were doing something forbidden added to the atmosphere.

Above all, it was the company, the friends I made. In some ways, the people who came to my parties were a sort of substitute for the family I never had. In the end, money's got nothing to do with it – what's more important is the kick you get out of giving everyone a good time as the perfect hostess.

So, let the party commence!

> ANY FORM OF ENTERTAINING INVOLVES EXPANDING A PRIVATE WORLD TO INCLUDE OTHERS. IT CALLS FOR AN EXTROVERT'S HEART AND AN INTROVERT'S SOUL.
> Martha Steward, *Entertaining,* 1983

CHAPTER 1

# PREPARING
# FOR YOUR PARTY

# Sending out invitations
The more indiscreet your party is likely to be, the more discreet your invitations should appear. There's no end to the people who are interested in sex parties but who are not what I would call bona fide guests. If you end up with a party infiltrated by journalists, wives, gatecrashers, Jack-my-Lads and policemen, it's bound to put a crimp on things.

So, here are examples of the correct and the incorrect way of wording an invitation.

CORRECT

AMBLESIDE AVENUE
LONDON SW16

*I will be holding my next party at 2.30 pm on 1 October. I hope you will be able to come.*

RSVP

DRESS: *Formal*

# Novelty invitations
Now and again, just for a laugh, I would make the invitations just a bit more interesting by using stationery used for children's parties. I always used to think that the pictures of girls and boys playing together were particularly appropriate for the occasion.

Most of those invited would put a large tick beside 'I WOULD LIKE TO COME'.

———— ◻ ————

# Ensuring the invitations reach the right hands
In the early days, I couldn't resist sending out invitations in cheerful, sexy pink envelopes. It was a mistake.

Very few wives are going to turn a blind eye to their husbands receiving that sort of mail. I soon got a desperate letter from this bloke saying, 'Whatever you do, send out your invitations in plain, buff envelopes.'

After that, I was more careful. I began

THE HOUSE OF 1,001 DELIGHTS
AMBLESIDE AVENUE
LONDON SW16

*You are Cordially Invited to a*

# SEX PARTY

*on 1 October with*

*Downstairs: food, drink, french maids, laughter, conversation and a sensational Live Lesbian Show and*

*Upstairs: June, Carla, Yvonne, Agatha, the Indian Princess and many other favourites.*

*Hope you can come – in more ways than one*

*Yours sexplicitly*

*Cynthia*

DRESS: *Optional*
UNDRESS: *Compulsory*

RSVP

INCORRECT

using large, buff envelopes of the type used for bills and circulars. My final precaution was to get a friend to typewrite the labels so that my invitations arrived looking like a note from the council. So far as I know, none of the wives suspected anything.

———— ◻ ————

# Presenting the correct image of yourself in your stationery
I've always been kinky for nice notepaper and, even during the days when I was running a brothel in Great Portland Street, I used to take care that I presented myself correctly in print.

'J. Mansell and Associates, Business Consultants', my printed writing-paper used to read. It was respectable and true – after all, it was a business and we did consult, after a fashion.

Recently, I've become more open with my stationery. My cards read Madame Cynthia Payne, LV, and my writing-paper is decorated with appropriate pictures.

My advice to hosts and hostesses is to let your stationery reflect your character.

———————— □ ————————

# REPLYING TO INVITATIONS

• In my experience, a lot of people ignore the 'RSVP' on an invitation and just turn up. This is very annoying for a hostess for whom getting the right numbers is very important. Some of my men would ring up to accept and sometimes they would send me a note confirming that they hoped to come in more ways than one. On the whole, the men were never a problem – I knew the definite starters or those that sometimes said 'Yes' but couldn't get away for some reason or other. Usually, if I invited forty men, I would expect about twenty-five to turn up.

Women, on the other hand, were much less reliable. The nightmare was that the men would be there but there would be too few girls to go round. So, in the old days I always used to ring them before the party, sometimes on the actual morning of the party, to remind them that they were needed.

The rudest thing a woman can do is to accept an invitation and not turn up. Since I've become well known, I've received a large number of invitations to all sorts of parties and film premières and I always try to give a definite answer as to whether I can make it or not – it can be a real let-down for a party if an important guest fails to turn up.

To....The Doctor....
Here is an invitation to
A Party
At..Ambleside Avenue, Streatham
Date..22nd July...Time..1:00.pm.
From...Cynthia......Tel:.....

REPLY

Dear....Cynthia....
Thank you so much for the
invitation to your party.
☑ I would like to come
☐ I won't be able to come
From...A, Doctor....

J. MANSELL AND ASSOCIATES
BUSINESS CONSULTANTS
11/89 GREAT PORTLAND STREET
LONDON W1N 5RA

It was the same with my parties. If I told the men that a certain very popular girl was going to be there and she wasn't, it could put a real damper on things.

□

# THE QUESTION OF DRESS •

Personally, I think it's important if you're giving a party to insist that people dress nicely – in fact, I used to make it a condition that a man shouldn't turn up sloppily dressed in jeans. For my kind of party, you had to be in casual wear or a suit – and most of the men wore suits. After all, the girls had gone to a lot of trouble to look pretty so why shouldn't the men show their respect by making a bit of an effort?

# FINDING YOUR FEMALE GUESTS •

You'll be wanting a special type of girl for your party if, as at my parties, there's as much activity upstairs as there is downstairs. They're not what you'd call real prostitutes, they're more like good-time girls, who are prepared to give value for money and enjoy themselves as well.

If you've got a bit of time, you'll need to buy some contact magazines and follow up a few likely ads. Then, once you're in touch with a girl and you've got to know her, ask her about her friends. Almost always, she has the telephone numbers of a few like-minded girls. In no time, you'll have a female guest list, the envy of every hostess in the neighbourhood.

In fact, once you get a reputation as a party giver, you'll discover that finding girls is no problem. The police used to be obsessed with this question.

'Where did you find the girls?' they used to ask me.

'I never had to find them,' I would reply. 'They found me.'

□

# EXTENDING YOUR MOST POPULAR GIRLS AN OPEN INVITATION •

One of the most important pieces of advice I can give to the serious partygoer is: when you discover a new girl who's really popular with the men, grab her telephone number as soon as possible. There's nothing that makes a party go better than nice, lively girls. But, time and time again, I've found that the best girls have come to one of my parties, made a few contacts of their own, and have never been seen again. For all that I know, they've set up their own parties. It can be a bit discouraging for a hostess if she finds that all her work in introducing a nice girl on to the party circuit is in vain.

Men like to see their favourites again and, if there's too much of a turnover on the female side, they tend to feel a bit unsettled. So, try to get a balance between the new blood and the regulars.

There's nothing that makes a party go better than nice, lively girls.

# MAKING CONTACT WITH NEW GUESTS •

Many magazines exist to help the enterprising party lover who wishes to meet like-minded people. Advertisers in these magazines tend to use their own particular turn of phrase, which can sometimes be confusing for the beginner and can lead to embarrassing misunderstandings.

Here is a list of some of the terms which do not mean what they say:

TVs WELCOME does *not* mean 'Bring along a television so that we can both enjoy *The Price is Right* together.'

HAS GOOD 'O' LEVELS does *not* necessarily mean that the advertiser is well educated, in the academic sense at least. Nor does the slightly rarer HAS GOOD 'A' LEVELS.

OVER-KNEE GAMES do *not* include indoor high jump.

FRENCH, GREEK, GERMAN, ENGLISH and ROMAN *rarely* have anything to do with nationality.

DIY does *not* involve a Black and Decker Workmate.

WATERSPORTS do *not* refer to Dive for the Penny or Water Polo.

NAPPY TRAINING is *not* an invitation to bring along slightly damp toddlers.

ENJOYS WRITING OF HER SAUCY ADVENTURES is *unlikely* to be *The Famous Five Go to Smugglers' Cove.*

> THERE IS NO GREATER OPPORTUNITY TO SHOW GOOD TASTE – OR BAD – THAN IN THE TYPE OF NOTEPAPER WE USE.
> Lady Troubridge, *The Book of Etiquette,* 1926

# MAKING CONTACT THROUGH THE POST: A CORRESPONDENCE COURSE

• Once you become a successful hostess, you'll find that all sorts of people write to you in the hope of being invited to a party or of being taken on as a slave. As these few extracts from letters sent to me prove, a lot can be learnt from the way each potential guest presents himself in his first letter to you.

---

*Dear Hostess,*

*I suppose that's how you would like to be addressed anyway.*

*I write to you in the hope of getting your attention though I do realise it is not going to be easy.*

*It is for sometime now, that I've been feeling the need of being taught some respect towards the female sex, for which I did not have much in the past. Perhaps you could enjoy doing that.*

■ *The forward slant of the writing and the tone of this letter suggest that the correspondent is uneasy and perhaps even slightly aggressive in his approach.*

---

*Above all I love fun and gardening. If my fun loving is nearly as good as my gardening it will be perfection. I grow the most beautiful exotic plants, with flowers very few people have seen before. I would supply the plants, seeds, and materials your*

■ *Again, a slight forward slant, but this letter shows more maturity and a distinct sense of humour. The interest in gardening is an excellent sign.*

---

*I would be most grateful to attend one of your parties they sound so friendly and relaxed, with no pressure put on anyone to do anything so civilised.*

■ *Although the writing here is of a man who may have been too young for my parties, he sounds pleasant, easygoing and attractively honest.*

---

*again, you are like Freddie Laker, her down one minute and up the next. why not. good for you, I can't see any thing wrong in what you are doing, whats better than sex.*

■ *This letter of support is clearly from an older man who is looking for liberation in his private life and is quite determined to find it.*

---

**I WOULD LIKE TO MAKE LOVE TO YOU**

■ *This less sophisticated approach is one that the hostess would be wise to ignore.*

---

*I have a very nice French maids outfit in hat wedlock, and shoes stockings, suspenders, and knickers and a lovely long Brown wig which you can dress me in.*

■ *The potential french maid very often has a tidy, controlled hand. This writer had a clear idea of what he needed, although the handwriting suggests that he may have been rather young.*

---

*Although enjoying the companionship of married life, I have not been offered sex for several years and consequently for most of the time, I suffer from strong yearnings and firey loins. yet, strangely, I do not seek sympathy, nor yet another woman on which to vent my pent-up lust, but rather yearn for the firm attentions of a beautiful mistress. She, without resorting to brash scolding, can nevertheless both tantalise and tease my frailty feelings by using her female power on the curious fringe of my sex life.*

■ *A confident and mature hand here indicates an older man who will be refreshingly direct and straightforward in his needs.*

*for the most part I agree with all that you are doing & wish you continued success & good helth (cheers) and I hope that you may find time to awnswer my letter so once more Good Luck as I must go now as I am a man of fairly few words & have run out of things to say.*

■ Not all potential guests find it easy to put their feelings on paper, yet manage to get their basic message through all the same.

*about all evil ways you have taken, living indecent life, running sex parties against Christ Jesus. If I may ask you do you know why you were created? I make it very clear to you that you were not born to establish Love Inns, rather you were born to serve your God through Jesus Christ who came to this world many years ago because*

■ This carefully written letter surprisingly failed to mention whether the writer wished to be invited to a party.

*Gardening is not my strong-point, but I can mow lawns, trim flower beds, and dig-out weeds. I am, however, fairly handy, both inside and outside!*

■ The subtle, slightly saucy joke is always nice in a letter, although this man's lack of gardening experience finally counted against him.

*RIGHT. YOU SHOULD GET THE O.B.E. MY DEAR LADY. I THINK OF YOU AS LOVELY AUNT. HELPING PEOPLE. WITH THEIR PROBLEMS I HOPE YOU CAN KEEP UP THE GOOD WORK, PTO.*

■ This careful, well-spaced writing indicates a solitary, perhaps rather lonely, man in his sixties. He may be looking for companionship rather than the traditional party-going activities.

*Mistress. What kind of things did you do to your last slave if you don't mind my asking?*

■ The handwriting here suggests extreme shyness and nervousness. The hostess may have considerable difficulty in bringing this guest out of himself at a party.

*I will perform any duties for you no matter how humiliating or degrading. I have been a slave to a very dominant lady in the past. I am experienced in washing clothes, dishes, hoovering, dusting, ironing, scrubbing floors, cleaning the toilet, bathroom, making beds etc. With my last Mistress I used to work all day and be chained up in the evening. Please, please I beg of you most Gracious Mistress allow me the chance to prove myself to you.*

■ Closed-up, forward handwriting normally reveals a closed-up, possibly frustrated character. This correspondent was perhaps a little too eager for his own good.

*May I state that I am warm hearted, easy-going, courteous, polite, respectful and am rather submissive to females. I have a good sense of humour and have indeed a longing to be near a ladies legs and feet! I am fun loving and love to be given duties*

■ My would-be slave here seems to be an outgoing, relaxed character. The rounded script suggests strong female characteristics in the writer.

```
I am well prepared to do anything you would like me
to do for you, with nothing in return except that
I would love to have a nice but quite time with
you ,no rush or panic,just relaxation and exciting
time and mutual satisfaction for both of us.
I am very discreet,clean,broadminded and I keep
my privacy just for myself .
```

■ The typewritten note is rather too formal for my liking and indicates a considerable lack of self-confidence, which may eventually pose problems for the hostess.

11

It's compli-cated, it's tiring and it's often rather messy. Requiring guests to eat complicated food like asparagus can really slow a party down.

# FOOD AND THE BUSY HOSTESS

• Personally, I think that nobody can cook a complicated meal and also entertain. Preparing and serving a meal is so time-consuming that, if I had to do that as well as be a good hostess, I'd be too knocked out to enjoy the party – and what would be the point of that?

So, my advice to a partygiver who wants to produce a big meal is quite simple – get someone in to do it. You'll have your hands full looking after the more interesting side of the party.

□

# SOME NOTES ON CUISINE

• I don't think men are that interested in food if there's crumpet around. At my parties, I used to get my slaves to prepare a few sandwiches for when people arrived and leave it at that. On the other hand, when a man's just come down from being upstairs, he's often a bit peckish.

## Poached Eggs à la Cynthia

I've tried a few different dishes for when the men have finished upstairs and need their strength building up – soup, fish, fried eggs and so on – but nothing has ever been as popular among my older men as my most famous dish, poached eggs. I like to think that, after all the publicity surrounding my trial, a couple of poached eggs is about the sexiest food a hostess can give her guests!

## Streatham Spuds

There's nothing like having a few big baked potatoes in the oven to be served up with butter. The police on their latest raid had just arrested me and were standing around before taking me down to the police station. I could tell that they were just waiting for me to say something incriminating. As they led me away, I suddenly shouted out, 'Oh I forgot, I forgot –' and the coppers all looked expectantly at me. 'The potatoes are in the oven. I'll be back in an hour – help yourselves to a big knob of butter!'

IT ISN'T THE *MENU* THAT MATTERS, IT'S THE *MEN YOU* INVITE.

Rose Henniker Heaton, *The Perfect Hostess*, 1931

## CHAPTER 2

# THE
# SERVANT
# PROBLEM

# FINDING HELP AROUND THE HOUSE •

Anyone who has ever held a party will know the work involved in preparing the place for it and getting ready for a sex party is no different. The last thing you need, if you want to be at your best as a hostess, is a long list of chores, ranging from preparing the sandwiches to making sure that the striptease artiste knows the address to come to. If you happen to be wealthy, then you can hire a servant, but if you're not, there's only one solution to your problem; *find yourself a slave*.

I first started using slaves when I was running the brothel in Great Portland Street. What with running the business – making sure the girls were there, booking the men in, chatting to them in the kitchen when one of the girls was behind schedule – the last thing I needed was to

*I find I can tell almost as soon as I meet a man whether he's potentially slavish.*

have to do the housework. It was then that a male friend of mine came up with the answer: 'Why don't you advertise for a manservant?'

'Don't be daft,' I replied. 'I don't want to pay anyone to come in.'

'You won't have to,' he said. 'Put the advertisement in and you'll have plenty of people who'll answer.'

So, very sceptically, I put an ad in a magazine. It read:

STRICT MISTRESS wishes to meet Gentleman who is willing to do housework, odd jobs about the house. Gardening an advantage.

With that one advert, the floodgates opened – I had literally hundreds of letters. Half the men in the country, it seemed, wanted to be a slave. It was this way that I met Slave Rodney, a married man who became my devoted slave for twenty years until he died, and Mitch, my Squadron Leader. It turned out that Mitch wasn't what you would call a proper slave – he only answered the ad to get near a woman – but he became one of my closest friends.

———————— □ ————————

# HOW TO TELL IF A SLAVE IS SUITABLE •

When advertising for your slave, remember that, while there are lots of men who like to be bossed around, there are very few who make really useful slaves around the house.

For a start, you should probably avoid men who want to dress up as maids, although they can be useful for the party itself. When it comes to housework and gardening, the average tranvestite is, frankly, a dead loss. He's really only interested in himself – what's happening to *him*, how much pleasure *he's* getting out of the situation.

Now the true slave would never be selfish. When he's near you, all that he ever wants is to please you. I used to get up in the middle of the morning when Slave Rodney was working in the house to find that everything in the place was

14

shining. The brasses had been cleaned, the tables dusted, the sun would be streaming through the windows. Slave Rodney could tell I was pleased (although it's a mistake to praise a slave too much) and that was all he wanted. When a slave is working for you, his whole reason for living is to make his mistress happy.

For this reason a good slave will never be jealous of other men. I was madly in love with a policeman for a while and I used to worry that Slave Rodney might be getting upset that I was so involved with another man. When I asked him about it, he seemed quite surprised.

'Why should I be?' he said. 'Just so long as I have a quarter of you, or even an eighth, or even the smallest fraction, I'll be happy.'

———— □ ————

# THE IMPORTANCE OF FOOTWEAR

• Managing a slave can be a complicated business. For instance, to make him feel good, you have to make him feel bad. To reward him, you have to punish him.

But the most important thing for a mistress to remember is that, if she wants to get and keep a slave, she must dress well, especially around the legs and feet. For the slave, you're the lady of the house, a superior, dignified, aloof sort of person and, to get the best out of him, that is the way you have to behave and to present yourself.

It was Slave Rodney who showed me how important footwear can be. Shortly after my kidney operation, I noticed that his housework was falling below his usually high standard. Not only that, he was moping about the place, and even snapped at me once or twice. Now when your slave starts answering back, you know something's wrong.

'What's up with you?' I asked. 'Why are you so bad-tempered these days?'

So he sat me down and explained the problem. 'I know you don't feel that well at the moment,' he said, 'but if I see you slopping around the house in those trousers and in those flat shoes, I'll go barmy.'

It was true that, since I had come out of

hospital, I had made less effort with my appearance when I was at home. I suppose, like all women, I was getting a bit slapdash. I said, 'I don't look that bad, do I?'

'Yes, you do,' he said, getting quite angry. 'I don't ask much when I come over here once or twice a week to keep your house clean and decorated. All I want is for you to look nice. If you can't be bothered to do your face or your hair, then for God's sake, take those awful slacks off and put a decent pair of high-heels on. That's not a lot to ask, is it?'

RIGHT          WRONG

I had to admit that it wasn't. Walking around the house in high-heels for a couple of hours may have taken it out of me a bit, but not nearly as much as doing my own housework would have. So very quickly I smartened myself up and Slave Rodney was back to his normal subservient self. If I hadn't taken myself in hand, I'm sure he would have lost interest and I would have lost the best slave (and one of the best friends) I ever had.

It may seem odd to some people that the slave needed to give the mistress a firm dressing-down for the mistress to be able to humiliate him to his own satisfaction, but that's just the way it worked.

## SEPARATING THE TRULY SLAVISH FROM THE MERELY SUBSERVIENT • These

days, I meet a lot of men who seem very determined to prove to me that they're as straight as a die, without a kink in them. Even doing something as simple as putting a coat around my shoulders, they'll say, 'Ooh, I'm not a slave, you know.' I'll usually reply, 'I never said you were,' and make a joke of it.

But the real joke is that a lot of men *are* slaves, without knowing it. I find I can tell almost as soon as I meet a man whether he's potentially slavish. There's something submissive about his attitude, a certain look in his eyes. He wants to be in your presence, to do things for you at the slightest opportunity.

## UNDERSTANDING YOUR SLAVE • There has been a lot of

interest in my slaves but for me there's nothing particularly strange about slavishness in a man. As we all know, men love rules – they live their lives by them. All that a slave does is to take obedience to rules one step further and to spend his time making a woman happy. It could hardly be less harmful, could it?

To be a good mistress, you must understand the needs of your slave and treat him accordingly. Slave Rodney's affection for high-heels, for example, had been an obsession which dated from puberty. He had been a servant in a hotel and one of the young maids had made him kneel at her feet, had placed her boot in his lap and made him clean it. He never forgot the experience.

Another of my most favoured slaves, Slave Philip, came to me after he had confessed his need to be humiliated to his wife. She had been so shocked by his confession that the physical side of their marriage ended at that point. Slave Philip was wonderful about the house, especially before a party, when he would hurry about the place helping the girls get ready, being generally bossed about and loving it. His particular need was to scrub the floor while stark naked, occasionally getting whacked on the arse by his mistress if he was slacking.

Then again, there are some slaves who are well over the top and who want you to do things that no self-respecting mistress would agree to. My advice to the average hostess would be to avoid kinkiness. Find yourself a slave who's a good worker and who'll be satisfied with straightforward humiliation at the end of the day. That way, everyone's happy.

———— □ ————

## HOW TO BEHAVE LIKE A MISTRESS • Don't let anyone kid

you that being a mistress is easy. As well as dressing for the part, you have to act it out as well, finding one horrible thing after another for your slave to do, never letting up with your orders, humiliating and degrading all day. Sometimes it

# THE MISTRESS'S DOS AND DON'TS

DO *behave like a superior mistress as soon as you open the front door to your slave.*

DON'T *say 'Oh hello, Keith, tell me when you want me to start.'*

DO *feel free to work your slave hard throughout the day. If he's anything less than shattered when he gets back home to his wife, he'll feel let down.*

DON'T *tidy up a bit before he comes round because the place is in a mess.*

DO *insist on being called 'Madam' throughout the day.*

DON'T *forget to call him 'Slave Kevin' at every opportunity, with something of a supercilious sneer in your voice.*

DO *laugh harshly when he tries to please you.*

DON'T *smile affectionately or wink.*

DO *walk around the house briskly in your high-heels as if in a permanent state of anger.*

DON'T *allow yourself to relax in his presence – slaves should rarely, if ever, see their mistresses 'off duty'.*

DO *have a cane, belt or similar symbol of authority handy in case your slave needs punishing/rewarding.*

DON'T *tolerate the slightest hint of slackness or laziness. Act with rage if you find him relaxing.*

DO *remember not to start chatting to him like an old friend (even if he is one). He's here for hard work and humiliation, not small talk.*

DON'T *slip out of role, becoming yourself rather than the superior mistress. This would be like Lady Macbeth turning to the audience mid-performance and asking what the time was.*

DO *give your slave a break at tea-time but suggest it in the right way.*

DON'T *say 'How about some nice tea and toast?'*

DO *say 'Make me a cup of tea right now this instant, and some toast while you're about it. Oh, and make yourself a bit if you want but make sure you eat it in the servant's quarters. I don't want you anywhere near me.'*

DON'T *forget to let him eat his tea off the floor and, if you're in a good mood, put it in a dog bowl and chain him to the leg of the kitchen table. Slaves deserve a treat now and then.*

can be as exhausting as doing the housework itself.

The real problem for a mistress is when her slave is also her friend. If Slave Rodney and I were alone in the house, I used to find it difficult to keep up the act because he was a sweet man, very dear to me, and making him do unpleasant things, even though he wanted me to, never felt quite right. The solution to the problem was to get an audience in. I used to invite a few friends round on a Friday and show him off as he worked around the house and garden. That used to make it easier for me and more exciting for him.

———— □ ————

THE YOUNGER SLAVE • In my experience, you get your best domestic slaves from the slightly older bloke. I get a lot of letters from men in their twenties and early thirties who are already a bit slavish, but they tend to be a bit confused about what they want and, as a result, they're less useful about the house.

It was for this reason that one of my good friends, the Psychologist, never became a full-time slave. He replied to my advertisement for a slave, sending a photograph and a charming letter and, when he came for an interview, I liked him a lot. But Slave Rodney, who used to help me on these occasions, warned me that, nice and intelligent as the Psychologist was, he would be difficult to handle as a slave. He was about thirty-two and very deep, uncertain as to what exactly he wanted. We remained good friends in the early days and I used to cane him now and then. As it happened, he met a singer at about the time my name was getting in the papers and, since she seemed a bit wary of the publicity, he stopped coming to see me. So now he has to go elsewhere for his beatings.

THE MOST SUCCESSFUL EMPLOYER OF STAFF IS THE ONE WHO MAKES HERSELF *FELT* RATHER THAN SEEN OR HEARD.
*Debrett's Etiquette and Good Manners*, 1981

THE PART-TIME SLAVE • Because so many men have the potential for slavishness, you may find that you don't actually need to advertise for domestic help, that your slave is already living with you.

It took me some time to realize the fact that a lot of men don't realize this tendency within them, and it was Slave Rodney who pointed it out to me.

Mitch, my Squadron Leader, used to spend a lot of time in my house and, although we were great friends really, we used to have these terrible rows, like a husband and wife. Suddenly, for no reason at all, Mitch would be going out of his way to annoy me. He'd be aggressive, cantankerous, and it would always be at the worst moment. When I was ill in bed with my kidney trouble, he'd come prancing into the bedroom wearing a Hawaiian grass skirt and yashmak.

'Get out of here,' I used to shout. 'What do you think you're doing, coming in here like that? You look a right sight!'

We'd have a laugh but it used to aggravate me, a man prancing around in drag, bare-arsed and ridiculous, and in the middle of the morning.

'Don't you understand?' Slave Rodney said to me one day. 'He's doing it on purpose. He wants a good beating.'

And it was true. After I had sorted him out with a good whipping, Mitch used to be as good as gold.

'Call yourself a Squadron Leader,' I'd shout as I was beating him. 'You can't fly a kite, let alone an aeroplane.'

He'd laugh and say, 'You're absolutely right, Madam.'

'What would your officers think of you if they could see you now? What about those young men you used to train to fly Spitfires – what would they think of you? Trussed up like a chicken and getting a good hiding.'

'They'd think I was very stupid, Madam.'

'I should think they would do, you silly old fool.'

Of course, there's quite an art to beating. It's usually important for a girl not to leave marks – there's many a married man who's had some explaining to do as he's been putting his pyjama-bottoms on. The whip has to land precisely on the buttocks, not on the thighs and certainly not on the back or in the kidney region. Mitch used to help me there by putting a belt around himself to give me something to aim at so that, after a couple of years, I became very good at it.

It takes hard work and practice. But, after all, hard work never hurt anyone (except, in this case, the bloke on the bed).

———— □ ————

# THE CASE AGAINST ALLOWING YOUR SLAVE TO PAY YOU

• A lot of men are so grateful for the opportunity to serve a strict mistress that, after a day of hard work around the house and in the garden, they expect to have to pay you. It's an idea I've never quite been able to get used to – charging someone to do the work you'd normally pay for – and I've always resisted the temptation to make money out of it.

The reason for this is simple. If your slave is paying you, he's in control of the situation. He can refuse to come round if he's not in the mood or if it's inconvenient. But if you're allowing him to work for you free of charge, he'll be only too happy to fit in with your plans.

# ON KEEPING TWO SLAVES

• Once you have mastered the art of keeping a slave happy, you may like to try getting more than one to help around the house. As you'll find, if you're a good, strict mistress, there's no shortage of men prepared to scrub and clean all day in return for a bit of humiliation.

Although I've never been quite nasty enough to satisfy many slaves, I spent several happy years being looked after by Mitch and Slave Rodney. In fact, we used to have some good laughs about it.

Mitch was always a bit of a stirrer and he used to enjoy getting Slave Rodney into trouble with me, which, of course, is just what a slave wants. Now and then, Mitch would open the door to Slave Rodney in the morning with a real look of concern on his face. 'Get in quick,' he'd say. 'You better go and see Madam now. She's *furious* with you for being late…' And off we'd go for another day of domination and domestic chores.

Then Slave Rodney would enjoy bringing out the subservient side of Mitch. If the Squadron Leader was in one of his truculent moods Slave Rodney might say to him, with a little, knowing grin, 'Now don't you talk to Madam like that.'

'I'll talk to Madam how I jolly well like,' Mitch would answer.

'Right, that's it,' I'd say. 'I'm not putting up with that sort of talk. Get me the cane right now.'

# THE QUESTION OF DISCIPLINE • I've never really quite understood why some men like it. Now and then I'd ask Mitch, 'What do you want to be beaten like that for?'

'Why do women like babies?' he used to say.

'Well,' I'd say, 'at least a woman's got something at the end of it.'

'It's the same with a beating,' he'd reply, as if it were the most natural thing in the world. 'There's something at the end of that.'

And there must have been for him because, once I started beating Mitch on a regular basis, he completely changed. I had known

him for eight years and, although we were friends, he used to be very mean with money. Yet, in the first year that I started giving him beatings, he loaned me £4,000 to buy my house.

———— □ ————

# THE ORIGINAL FRENCH MAID • When I first started holding kinky parties for kinky people, I was contacted by this bloke who was a transvestite who wanted to come along to the parties in full female gear.

'Don't you think it would be a good idea,' he said when I met him, 'if I came along as a French maid – the original French maid.'

I had my doubts at first, but then I thought of the cost of hiring someone to help. Here was this man desperate to help for nothing – anything to get an entrée into my parties. So I agreed.

At first, I thought I had made a terrible mistake. He looked a right idiot when he arrived for his first party. A man of fifty, togged up with a blond wig, a black satin outfit and fish-net tights.

'Oh dear, oh dear,' I said to him, 'You remind me of my Aunt Mabel.'

# ENCOURAGING YOUR FRENCH MAID TO ACT HER AGE • Many French maids go a bit mad to start with and want to dress up like a tart. The hostess needs to discourage this tendency with as much tact as possible. Say something along the lines of, 'For heaven's sake, Peter, you look absolutely ridiculous. You're too old to be acting the blinking tart, and that's all there is to it.'

Quite soon, your French maid will get the message. My original French maid eventually abandoned his blond wig and, with a certain amount of reluctance, took to coming in a grey wig, which was more suitable for his age. He may not have looked the sexiest thing on high-heels, but at least he had a certain dignity to him.

CHAPTER 3

# GETTING
# IN THE
# PARTY MOOD

# BREAKING THE ICE AT PARTIES •

One of the reasons why my parties were so successful was that there was always a nice, free and easy atmosphere about them. If people wanted to go upstairs, nobody looked at them and said, 'Ooh, you can't go upstairs in this house, we don't do that sort of thing here.' I'm very easygoing in my speech so that no one was made to feel embarrassed by what they said or did; no one thought that they were taking liberties when they were being relaxed and natural – and, of course, they knew that whatever happened in my house, I wasn't going to sell them down the river.

# INTRODUCING GUESTS TO ONE ANOTHER •

A lot of men are shy, particularly when everyone else at a party seems to know one another. So, at my parties if I saw somebody on his own and looking a bit out of place, I'd chat with him for while. Then, if he happened to look at one of the girls and say, 'Oh, she's nice,' I'd sort of wink at the girl as if to say, 'Come and keep this one company because I've got to look after the drinks.' Soon after that, the exhibition would start and, once you've got a Dance of the Seven Veils going, shyness soon disappears.

> CAN ANYTHING IN THE WORLD BE NICER THAN A REALLY NICE GIRL?
> Mrs Humphrey, *Manners for Women*, 1987

# A NOTE ON BEING ARRESTED FOR 'CONTROLLING' AS A RESULT OF INTRODUCING GUESTS TO ONE ANOTHER •

Unfortunately, there are some people who think that if a hostess winks at a girl and introduces her to a man, then she's guilty of what the law calls 'controlling'. At my latest trial, the prosecution made a lot of this winking business – they said that I winked and everybody would go upstairs.

My answer to this was that I might well have winked as a couple went upstairs but then I'm always winking and I'm always introducing people to one another. That's what being a good hostess is all about.

So, unless you actually have policemen on the premises, don't be afraid to do a bit of winking.

—————— □ ——————

# HOW FRENCH MAIDS CAN LEND A HAND •

There's nothing like a bit of laughter at a party and I've found that having a couple of blokes dressed up as French maids, serving the guests

with drinks, can soon get everybody going. For the hostess, it's practical, for the guests, it's fun, and for the maids being ordered about the place by everyone, it's a real turn-on.

Of course, ideally, you want to get blokes who can look glamorous, with nice legs and so on, because they'll really try to look good. It's as if they're saying, 'Look, we're better than any woman.' And some of them are, when they're all dressed up.

———— □ ————

## SOME THOUGHTS ON RELAXING GUESTS AT AN ALL-DAY PARTY •

I suppose I first got into the habit of chatting all the time when I was running a brothel. A lot of the men who rang the bell would be so nervous and shy that by the time I opened the door, they'd be half-way down the stairs. I learnt very quickly that you should open the door with a big smile

on your face, and then you have to do all the talking until they begin to feel more at ease.

'Come into the kitchen,' I'd say, as if I were welcoming them into my own home. 'I'll make you a cup of tea. She'll be with you soon.'

Then they might get a bit nervous to think there's another man in the flat.

'She's not going to be too long, is she?' they'd say.

'No, no. Have a cup of tea and look at my photograph albums.'

Because even then I used to enjoy taking photographs all the time and the albums, which had lots of photographs of the girls, really began to revive their interest. So, the bloke had his cup of tea and we'd chat, maybe for half an hour, at the end of which he was relaxed, he was interested and he trusted me. And by then the girl was ready.

It was the best training that any hostess could hope for.

One of the reasons why my parties were so successful was that there was always a nice free and easy atmosphere about them.

23

# SOME USEFUL HOUSEHOLD APPLIANCES

### TALCUM POWDER AND BABY OIL

*These toiletries, used imaginatively by the artists helped by a member of the audience, have brought many a striptease exhibition to a rousing climax. Note: use either the powder or the oil, not both – mixed together they form a sticky coating which is less conducive.*

### THE CARPET – BEATER

*This simple household object can give certain guests untold pleasure, although the conventional schoolmaster's cane is generally preferred.*

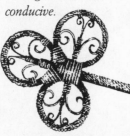

### THE COLLAR, CHAIN AND DOG BOWL

*Available at any good* pet shop, these items are a never-ending source of satisfaction for the average slave.

### THE VACUUM CLEANER

*Who would have thought that a simple vacuum cleaner would be useful for a party? Yet one of my most successful and best-known social occasions – stringing up a bank manager at his request and inviting other guests to pelt him with filth – would have been nothing without this device.*

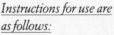

*Instructions for use are as follows:*
**1** String up your bank manager.
**2** Remove the contents of the bag (for best effect, try to save up several weeks' worth of household dust).
**3** Add water, stirring vigorously.
**4** Pelt the bank manager.

## THE FLOWER – HANGER

*Following my last raid, there were those who thought that this household object was used for kinky practices! It was only when we showed it being put to its proper use, with lovely spider plants and canary creepers cascading from the ceiling, that it became clear what it was actually for. Flowers are always pleasant at a party and this container will show the right hanging plants to advantage.*

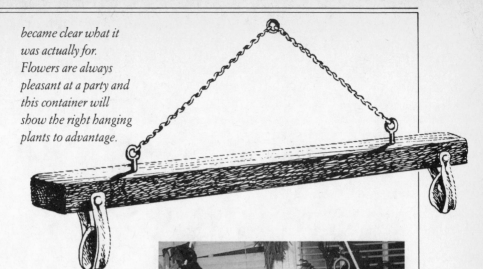

## THE CLOTHES – HORSE

*One of my slaves made this useful device in his loft at home, telling his wife that he was building a mast for his sailing-boat. It took six months to complete and, for reasons of security, had to be brought over piece by piece to Ambleside Avenue and assembled in situ. It seemed a lot of trouble for a clothes – horse that needed to be used for restraining a slave who needed disciplining only now and then.*

*Not everyone has access to a handyman, so you may decide to use an ordinary sturdy ironing-board for the same purpose (The iron can be useful, too!)*

25

# THE HOSTESS'S TEN COMMANDMENTS

**I** Thou shalt not arrive at the party with a wife, husband, friend, friend of a friend, business associate, a couple of blokes I just met in the pub, mother, father, brother, or minder unless they have been specifically invited.

**II** Thou shalt declare thy profession (e.g. policeman, journalist, film producer) at the door when relevant.

**III** Thou shalt not go upstairs with anyone before circulating, chatting and behaving in a civilized way for at least ten minutes.

**IV** Thou shalt not make unnecessary comments about the performers while an exhibition is in progress.

**V** Thou shalt not attempt to stage an exhibition downstairs without first obtaining the permission of both the hostess and your partner.

**VI** Thou shalt use the Bathroom, Kitchen and Mirror Room for their proper purposes only.

**VII** Thou shalt not attempt to jump the queue on the stairs, however great thy need.

**VIII** Thou shalt treat the French maid with due respect, even if he does look a chump in a blond wig and wobbly high-heels.

**IX** Thou shalt not carry hidden cameras or notebooks, neither shalt thou be wired for sound.

**X** Thou shalt adjust thy clothing before leaving.

CHAPTER 4

# SOME FAVOURITE PARTYGOERS OF THE PAST

# MITCH, THE SQUADRON LEADER

• I first met Mitch through a contact magazine. I was looking for a slave at the time but Mitch, although he was occasionally slavish, basically just wanted a bit of fun. Very soon, he became a regular visitor and a really good friend. It turned out that his wife had died ten years previously. They had had a very close marriage – 'She never once refused me,' Mitch always used to say – so when she died in her mid-forties, without the slightest warning, he just went barmy. Apparently, he became very lonely waking up in the bed, day after day, with no woman by the side of him and, according to him, that's when he became kinky.

He locked himself away in Purley, occasionally visiting massage parlours but rarely going out. Without regular sex, he let himself go. He had all his teeth taken out because he hated going to the dentist.

'Why did you do that?' I asked him once. 'You look awful. Why didn't you at least get a denture?' 'Oh I wasn't bothered with a denture,' he said, 'I thought, who's going to want me now?'

That was why it was so lucky we met. Mitch couldn't believe that here was a woman who didn't want younger men around her, who actually liked the older man. And, although I didn't go to bed with him sexually, he did attract me – like a father.

Over the years, we became very close. He used to dress up in women's clothing – an evening gown, or, as I described earlier, in a grass skirt, complete with a yashmak over his face. He was very interested in bondage and I always thought that the whipping and beating resulted from a guilt complex, connected with the death of his wife. The dressing up I could understand

> UNDERSTAND YOUR BODY AND ALLOW
> IT TO ENJOY THE RIGHT OF SPEAKING WITH
> AS MUCH FREEDOM AND RESTRAINT AS YOU
> WOULD WITH WORDS.
> Sol Chaneles, *The New Civility,* 1973

– he loved everything about women and it was almost a substitute for not having a woman about the place all the time. He used to say that a man without a woman is nothing, that women are like flowers – if you don't look after them they'll wither and die. That was why he hated blue films – he thought that they degraded women, and maybe he was right.

———— ◻ ————

# AGATHA, THE WIFE-SWOPPER

• Although she was hardly a beauty and no longer exactly in the first flush of youth, Agatha was always one of the most popular women at my parties. She liked all the socializing and party-going downstairs, of course, but upstairs was what she was really interested in. Yet, to look at her, no one would believe that Agatha was a raver. She looked as prim and proper as a West Country shopkeeper, which, as a matter of fact, she was.

I met her after I had put an ad in a contact magazine – 'KINKY PEOPLE WANTED FOR KINKY PARTIES' – and did she fit the bill! She and her husband had been wife-swappers in their village but, because it was a small community and she was well-known through her shop, they decided it was a bit risky, so they started coming to my parties.

In those days, there was no money involved but Agatha and the two other women who usually came were there for the pleasure and the laughs. She was mad for sex, this Agatha, and her husband used to be quite happy to see her go upstairs with one man after another. When, in the early 1970s, girls started getting paid for it, she decided to charge as well – it was not that she needed the money, but it added to the thrill. She changed, became more confident. Once she had thought a bloke was doing her a favour to take her to bed; now they were actually paying her. So, every time I held an afternoon party, she'd shut up shop early and hotfoot it up to London. It was partly the intrigue that excited her, the double life – that and the sex, of course. She told me that coming to my parties had actually saved her marriage.

MITCH, THE SQUADRON LEADER

I sometimes wonder how many Agathas there are all over the country, leading quiet, frustrated lives, running village shops or whatever, doing a bit of wife-swapping now and then. It's a pity there aren't more parties like mine to give them a bit of freedom to express themselves, like Agatha did.

□

THE MAJOR • One of my regulars in the early days was the Major, a very dominant little man in his sixties. When he came to the parties, he used to relive his youth in a rather peculiar way.

Apparently, the most exciting moments of his life as a young man were when he was serving as a junior officer in the army during the war. He used to watch the WAAFS in a nearby barracks, washing-up and doing their exercises. In the summer-time, they used to wear these little khaki shorts, through which he could just see their knickers.

It must have been quite an experience because, thirty-five years later, he still found nothing more exciting than to act it out over and over again. However, as time took its toll,

he needed more stimulation: whereas one pair of knickers under the pair of shorts was enough when he was a young man, now he needed six pairs, peeled off slowly by the girl, one by one, as she waltzed around the room, occasionally being given orders by the Major. The girl always had to start with the genuine 1941 vintage pair of khaki shorts which, without fail, the Major brought with him. We used to laugh like mad about it, but only after he had gone. We'd never want to upset the Major.

□

THE SWINGING POLICE-MAN • Some men live for years in the closet, married, but with the sexual side of their life almost completely suppressed. This was the case with Copper Henry, an ex-policeman I met during the 1960s, who has since died. He had quite a stable marriage, with two daughters, but behind the respectability, he was very frustrated. All that changed after he and I took a brief but eventful trip to Hamburg in 1969.

He saw everything, from couples dancing topless at a nightclub to a totally authentic, all-night Roman orgy at a local hotel. At first, he

29

was flabbergasted – 'If this was England, I'd have to get them raided,' he said at one point – but, very quickly the true Copper Henry came out, and he really started to enjoy himself.

As he admitted himself, those few days changed his life – they turned his head completely. After his return, he was on the look-out for new experiences, forever inquiring when the next party was going to be. I have no doubt that being liberated during his last years made him a happier man.

——————— □ ———————

**T**HE DOCTOR • The Doctor is one of my old friends, a charming, well-educated man now in his fifties, who was the life and soul of many of my parties.

The Doctor's great interest in life was taking part in exhibitions. What a performer that man was! He was never happier than when rolling around on the floor stark naked with a girl, watched by a group of appreciative onlookers.

In the early days, he used to find one of the girls for his exhibition, paying well over the odds for the pleasure – five or six luncheon vouchers, it used to cost him.

Then, at one party, something marvellous happened. There was a lovely young oriental girl there for the first time. The Doctor and she got together and, miracle of miracles, they discovered that they shared a definite interest in the performing arts.

After that, hardly a party during the 1970s went by without the Doctor and his girlfriend putting on this fantastic exhibition. On and on, they used to go. In the living-room, in the hall, on the top landing (a great asset when people were getting bored waiting in a queue). Of course, it used to be a blooming nuisance – you'd find yourself tripping over them when you were trying to get someone a drink – but, on the whole, they were great for any party. Nothing helps to break the ice like a good exhibition.

CHAPTER 5

# CHOICE
# ENTERTAINMENTS
## FOR YOUR GUESTS

# ON PROVIDING AN EXHIBITION FOR YOUR GUESTS •

There's really nothing like a bit of entertainment to make your guests feel at ease and get the party going with a swing – in fact, if you hint that there's going to be a bit of a cabaret when you invite them, you'll probably be guaranteed a packed house. Soon your regular guests will know what to expect and you'll have no trouble in getting a full house from then on.

First of all, you want to give people a bit of time to arrive, settle down, have a drink and meet each other.

When they are all relaxed on a comfortable sofa or chairs, dim the lights, turn the music up – and let the exhibition commence.

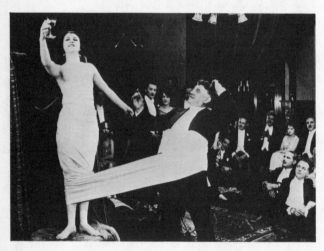

# THE STRIPTEASE •

A lively girl who knows what she's doing and with the right music can really produce a happy atmosphere at a party.

At Ambleside Avenue, they used to prepare in the kitchen and just when everything was perfect – the music, the lights, everyone waiting in anticipation – in they'd come.

It's particularly good if the girl can bring a tin of talcum powder with her, or some baby oil. Then, in the middle of the act, when she's got down to topless, she can perhaps pick the oldest chap in the audience, give him the oil to rub over her or the talcum powder to shake all over her. That's caused lots of laughs in my time

– and the men love it.

Ideally, you should have a couple of striptease girls who are really attractive and fun. By the time they've finished, the party's really on its way.

# THE LIVE LESBIAN SHOW •

A lot of people like to see a live lesbian show but, in my experience, it needs to be very, very good to make it worth while. Mitch used to say that it wasn't really worth the bother because after all they're only just lying there sort of caressing, whereas with, say, a Dance of the Seven Veils at least the girls are moving about a bit.

The other problem with the live lesbian show was that, if you were going to put on two exhibitions, you would end up paying for three girls – a stripper and the lesbians. So, in the end, I started putting on two really good striptease artistes – they were just as popular as the lesbians and were more cost-effective.

# THE STRIPOGRAM ARTISTE •

I know that kissograms, stripograms and the like are very popular at parties these days but, in my view, they're something of a last resort. Of course, some of the girls are quite attractive but they don't stay for more than half an hour and after that it's off to the next appointment.

There's nothing more disappointing for a group of men than to see a girl doing a striptease, to have the atmosphere brought up high with a really good act; they like her, they start chatting to her – because for them, she represents sex and men just love talking to stage stars, chorus girls and that sort of thing – and then she says, 'Well, I'll be off now.' All the men look at her as if to say, 'Going already?' and you can see the disappointment in their eyes, hear it in their voices. It's a real anticlimax.

So, my advice is to avoid the stripograms and get a couple of good-time girls who'll strip and then stay for the rest of the party.

# ON DISCOURAGING YOUR GUESTS FROM GOING UPSTAIRS BEFORE THE EXHIBITION HAS COMMENCED •

In the beginning I didn't let anyone go upstairs until after the exhibition. Girls used to come up to me and say, 'But he wants to go upstairs now, he doesn't want to wait until after the exhibition because then all the bedrooms will be full – he's not interested in the exhibitions.' But I used to stick to my guns because in those days I believed in the gearing up to it, the excitement, the *anticipado* – I thought it all added to the party.

After a while, I realized that the men were geared up already by the time they arrived. They had been thinking about this sex party for days, so, by the time they got to Ambleside Avenue, all sexed up, they just didn't want to wait. They saw the girls and wanted to go straight upstairs. Then again, there were only four bedrooms and they did get very busy later on. Some men didn't like queuing on the stairs for too long.

I couldn't handle that in the beginning – after all that trouble getting a nice lesbian show or stripper, all they wanted to do was go upstairs – but, after a few parties, I let them do what they liked.

Sometimes they'd come down at about 3.30 and say, 'Where's the exhibition?' I'd tell them they'd missed it and they would be disappointed, but it was their fault for being so eager.

———————— □ ————————

# ON MOVING THE EXHIBITION UPSTAIRS TO ACCOMMODATE GUESTS WHO COULDN'T WAIT •

Because so many of my men were missing the exhibition by going upstairs soon after they arrived at the early parties, I hit on the idea of holding a second showing of the exhibition at the top of the stairs on the landing. Unfortunately, it never really caught on. Some of the men had already seen it once downstairs and the rest had their minds on other things.

# THE PERFECT HOSTESS WILL ALWAYS BE PREPARED TO JOIN IN THE FUN

The best way to make the atmosphere at your party relaxed and happy is to be relaxed and happy yourself, and this means participating as much as you can. Although I've never actually gone upstairs at one of my parties – I'm needed downstairs organizing and helping to keep everything going – I once put on a bit of an exhibition.

It was in 1978, just three months before my trial. I was out on bail, I'd just had my kidney operation and, although I knew that I'd almost certainly be in prison by the end of the year, I felt wonderfully well. I was dancing at this party we were having and suddenly, on an impulse, I just stripped to the waist.

The people in the room couldn't believe their eyes. Some of them rushed out of the kitchen, shouting, 'Come and look at this – Cyndy's stripping!' They'd never seen me actually do that at one of my own parties.

One moment, I was dancing topless with this bloke, the next, nearly every couple did it and it ended up a really good party.

I suppose that the girls had never stripped downstairs because they'd thought they had to keep it respectable but, once the hostess had done it, they were all keen to go one better. 'If she can do it,' they were thinking, 'we're younger than her, prettier than her, maybe even got a better bust than her' (mind you, they'd have had a job, even at that age). So why not?

> YOU SHOULD PROVIDE TWO KINDS OF AMUSEMENTS. THE FIRST SHOULD CONSIST OF DIVERSIONS IN WHICH EVERY INDIVIDUAL ACTUALLY PLAYS A PART, AND IN THE SECOND THE COMPANY WILL MERELY LOOK ON. THE FIRST SHOULD PREDOMINATE, BUT THE SECOND IS VALUABLE AS IT PROVIDES A FORM OF REST FOR SPECTATORS.
> *How to Make an Evening Go*, 1925

As it happens, I've never been tempted to strip since then, but there's nothing that gets people more relaxed than seeing the hostess joining in the fun. So, no matter what sort of party you're holding, some kind of striptease, if possible involving yourself, is an absolute must. Otherwise people just sit about, they drink, they get bored, they drink some more and that's the end of your party.

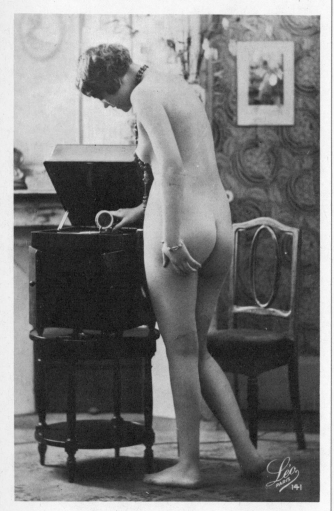

## MUSICAL INTERLUDES AT A LESS CONVENTIONAL PARTY • Frankly, if sex is on the menu, no one's going to take a blind bit of notice of any music for the first two hours of your party.

I tried it a few times and hired a bloke with a guitar whom I had found busking in the Underground. It never worked as well as I hoped it would. He'd get really choked that he was playing away and no one was interested – all the men wanted to do was get with the birds and go upstairs. But we found that when quite a few of them had left and the rest of them were sitting round the fire, despunked, then his music was really nice.

If the musician wasn't around, I'd put on one of my tapes, something easygoing and romantic – Johnny Mathis, Nat King Cole, Frank Sinatra – and sometimes one or two people would get up to dance.

————— □ —————

## THE PROGRAMME FOR A PERFECT AFTERNOON PARTY • No two parties at Ambleside Avenue were ever the same because there were always surprises, some pleasant (an unscheduled live show by the Doctor and his girlfriend which lasted over half an hour), some not so pleasant (an unscheduled visit by forty members of the Vice Crime Squad).

But, generally speaking, the timing would go something like this:

| | |
|---|---|
| 1.00 | *The first guests arrive* |
| 2.00 – 3.00 | *Drinks and sandwiches (occasional visits upstairs)* |
| 3.00 | *The last girls arrive* |
| 3.30 | *The exhibition (striptease or live lesbian show)* |
| 4.00 – 5.30 | *The guests go upstairs while, downstairs, there may be some dancing and chat, or perhaps the Doctor and his girlfriend would entertain us* |
| 4.30 | *The second exhibition* |
| 5.00 – 6.00 | *Some of the more energetic men would choose a second girl to go upstairs with* |
| 5.30 – 6.00 | *Refreshments – baked potatoes, poached eggs, a cup of tea* |
| 6.00 | *The guests depart* |

CHAPTER 6

# ETIQUETTE
## FOR THE
## PARTYGOER

# OBSERVING AN EXHIBITION

• It's exceedingly bad manners to allow your attention to wander during an exhibition, whether it's a Dance of the Seven Veils, a live lesbian show or a couple of guests enjoying themselves for the benefit of onlookers. The last thing performers need at a time when they need to concentrate is any kind of distraction.

This was brought home to me at one of my earliest parties. We were all enjoying an exhibition upstairs. One couple were performing on the bed and all around them, seated in a semicircle and sipping tea, were other gentleman guests. It was a lovely scene, very English in a way. Then suddenly someone started making a noise with his cup and saucer.

'Don't do that,' I said. 'It's nerve-wracking enough for the couple on the bed without you rattling away in the corner. If you want to make a noise like that, you can go downstairs.' That shut him up.

## POINT OF ETIQUETTE

*If you're lucky enough to be enjoying an exhibition, have respect for the performers – sit still and keep quiet.*

# TAKING PART IN AN EXHIBITION

• It's nice for a party to be well organized. If there's not a certain order to things, then guests might feel they could have been to any old orgy rather than to a lovely social gathering where sex happens to be on the menu.

For this reason, you should observe the correct procedure before indulging in an an exhibition. Nobody likes to be hurried and, if a couple are putting on an exhibition in the hall before guests have even had time to take off their coats, it can be quite off-putting at times.

So, remember to wait until the party is in full swing. Then, if so inclined, take your partner, dance closely to the music and, having received a 'Go ahead' wink from the hostess, you may proceed with the exhibition.

## POINT OF ETIQUETTE

*It is as impolite to start a performance before the other guests are ready as it would be to tuck into your meal at a dinner party before anyone else has sat down.*

# ENJOYING A QUICK ONE

• It may be your first time at a party like this. You may be nervous, tense. Even after the live lesbian show, you haven't quite got the courage to ask the girl of your choice upstairs. You help yourself to a whisky. You feel better. You have another, then one more for luck. *Now* you're ready for upstairs.

Except you're not. It's stupid as well as impolite to drink too much when you're at a sex party. During my years in the brothel, I've had to listen to countless men trotting out the old 'This has never happened to me before' excuse. I had one question: 'Have you been in the pub?' And the answer was always the same. They had needed the Dutch courage.

## POINT OF ETIQUETTE

*It's either booze or sex, not both. He who drinks downstairs is in for a small disappointment upstairs and so is his girlfriend.*

# THE PERILS OF OVER-ENTHUSIASM

• Something happens to a man when he's trying to get a girl to go to bed with him. He hangs around her, trying to be charming and cool and, more often than not, he's just unnatural. A man who's really nice when he's his normal self can look a right twit when he's trying to get his end away.

Unfortunately, the same is often true

THE MAN SHOULD INITIATE THE KISS WITH CARE SO THAT IF HE SHOULD AT ANY STAGE FEEL HIS KISS UNWELCOME TO THE LADY, HE WILL BE ABLE TO DRAW BACK. IT IS AN ART WHICH COMES WITH EXPERIENCE AND USUALLY ONE KNOWS IF THE WOMAN IS *FRIENDLY*.
Lady Penelope, *Etiquette Today*, 1982

when a girl fancies a bloke, as I know to my cost. In the past, I've lost men I've really wanted because I've run after them, doing everything for them, gushing and cooing rather than being my natural, direct self.

## POINT OF ETIQUETTE

*If you discover your Romeo or your Juliet, try to keep your emotions in check. Lose control and you'll lose your partner.*

# IN THE QUEUE ON THE STAIRS •

When a party is in full swing, occasionally there can be a certain amount of congestion on the stairs. If there was too much of a queue at one of my parties, I used to arrange an exhibition on the top landing but, even so, a few guests would become slightly impatient, particularly if they were raring to go.

Yet, however keen you are to get in the bedroom, you should never ever bang on the door or shout through the keyhole things like, 'How long are you going to be in there?' Any reasonably sophisticated guest will know that the girl will be doing her best and that, if she has run over the normal thirty minutes, then she's having difficulties of some sort. Now the last thing a couple having a problem on the bed needs is someone hammering on the door – if anything, it's going to slow him down and delay things even more.

## POINT OF ETIQUETTE

*Be patient at all times – if it's worth having, it's worth waiting for.*

# UPON DISCOVERING A SECRET DOUBLE MIRROR IN THE BEDROOM •

Double mirrors are popular in some quarters, a lot of guests enjoy the idea of putting on an exhibition without the noise and the jostle of people in the same room. Yet many others, and I sympathize with these people, don't like the idea of not knowing whether they're being watched or not.

When going upstairs at a party run by someone you don't know very well, it may be a good idea to look behind the pictures and mirrors to check for hidden spyholes.

## POINT OF ETIQUETTE

*Upon discovering that you may be observed upstairs, do not scream the house down. Merely cover the offending mirror or peephole with a towel or a pair of trousers.*

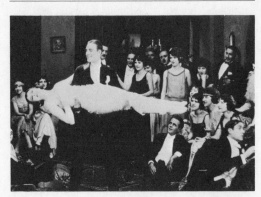

It's exceedingly bad manners to allow your attention to wander during an exhibition.

# LAYING BETS AT A PARTY •

There was one girl who used to come to my parties who was charming but very, very large. In fact, she was one of the biggest girls I've ever seen. For this reason, she was never the most popular of my girls but, since she was good company, I used to like inviting her.

On one occasion, I discovered that some of the guests were actually laying bets among themselves as to who would dare to go upstairs with her. I believe a fiver was the stake involved. She never knew about it, but I soon put a stop to that sort of nonsense. Once you start having those sorts of silly games at your parties, the atmosphere of warmth and trust soon goes out of the window.

## POINT OF ETIQUETTE

*It is very ill-mannered to laugh at or make money out of other people's misfortunes.*

# SAYING 'THANK-YOU' AFTER A PARTY •

One of the great pleasures of giving parties for men whose lives are perhaps a little bit dull away from Ambleside Avenue is in knowing that not only

# SOME USEFUL EXCUSES FOR TRICKY SOCIAL SITUATIONS

Everyone has experienced those embarrassing incidents that can happen at any party. Here are some essential get-out lines for the trickiest moments.

ON ARRIVING IN THE SAME COCKTAIL DRESS AS A MEMBER OF YOUR GOLF CLUB
*'No, no, I insist, Charles – shocking pink looks <u>much</u> better on you.'*

ON BEING DISCOVERED IN A COMPROMISING POSITION DURING A RAID BY THE VICE SQUAD
*'It's all right, officer, I'm just doing some upfront research for a major motion picture.'*

ON BEING TOO NERVOUS TO ACCEPT AN INVITATION TO PARTICIPATE IN AN EXHIBITION
*'Sshh. PC Perkins, Vice Squad. One word from you, Chummy, and it'll be six months for aiding and abetting. Move along there.'*

ON BEING INVITED UPSTAIRS BY SOMEONE YOU FIND RATHER UNATTRACTIVE
*'You'll have to excuse me but I sustained a sporting injury at an all-night orgy in Plaistow last night.'*

ON DISCOVERING THAT THE FRENCH MAID YOU HAVE ASKED UPSTAIRS IS YOUR BANK MANAGER
*'What a delightful surprise, Mr Williams. Now I know what's meant by "the bank that likes to say yes".'*

ON BEING ASKED IF YOU'D LIKE TO COME UPSTAIRS TO MAKE A SANDWICH
*'Excuse me, but the cuisine arrangements are not my responsibility.'*

ON A LUNCHEON VOUCHER BEING FOUND IN A BACK POCKET BY ONE'S WIFE
*'Yes, darling, it's what we businessmen call an executive perk.'*

have they had the sex, but they've also enjoyed a really nice day out. Even in my brothel days, it was never a question of them just arriving, seeing the girl and going – quite often they'd knock on my door and we'd sit around chatting over a cup of tea or a lager for most of the afternoon. For them, there was much more to it than simply the girls. It was an escape from the routine of their lives and I liked seeing them because, after a while, they became my friends. It was never just a business.

So, when they kissed me goodbye on the doorstep, I could often see in their eyes and hear in their voices that they had had a nice day and that they were fond of me.

That, for me, was 'thank you' enough, my reward. Of course, some men used to write saying that it had been a most enjoyable day or that Raksha the Indian girl was just as good as I'd said she would be – but normally the look on their faces was enough.

## POINT OF ETIQUETTE

*Gratitude, however expressed, is a must for all party guests.*

CHAPTER 7

# SOME WELL-KNOWN
# PARTY TYPES

# THE FIRST-TIMER • It's important for the hostess to realize that many of the men who say, 'Oh, I couldn't come to a party like that,' and, 'I certainly couldn't do that,' more often than not are really dying to do it but are too shy. Any serious partygiver should persist with this type because in the end he'll come along and, after he's lost his inhibitions, he'll have a wonderful time.

I remember a little bloke I met when he was in his fifties who just would not come to one of my parties. He was a quiet, disillusioned man, very sweet but unbelievably timid about women. I coaxed and I coaxed and, at long last, I managed to persuade him to come to a party. For a while, he stood about looking embarrassed and out of place. Eventually, I decided to shake him out of it. 'Are you going upstairs or what?' I said, and, a bit sheepishly, he did. After that, I couldn't keep him away – you could see the liberation on his face.

That's the way with the First-Timer. Give him a bit of a push and soon he'll be loving it.

PARTY TYPES

PARTY TYPES

THE WALLFLOWER

THE EXHIBITIONIST

# THE EXHIBITIONISTS • At a conventional party, the show-off is someone people tend to avoid; at a sex party, he or she is always popular. Because, although a striptease or a live lesbian show is enjoyable, there's nothing quite like a surprise, impromptu exhibition by a couple who happen to like performing before an appreciative audience.

Although talented exhibitionists were always welcome at my parties, the couple who guests used to like best was the Doctor and his lovely girlfriend. One moment they'd be dancing quietly with one another, the next they would be on the floor, in the hall, in the kitchen – anywhere but in the bedroom behind closed doors. They were such brilliant performers and they had such amazing stamina that nobody could fail to have a good time when they were around.

———— □ ————

# THE WALLFLOWER • If your parties are anything like mine, you'll find that you very rarely suffer the problem of guests standing around, feeling out of things. At a sex party, everybody tends to get involved – if they're not doing, they're watching, or maybe saving their energy for later.

There was one girl, a regular at the parties, who used to seem astonishingly shy. 'What's the matter with her?' the men used to ask, because she never talked, never laughed or joined in. Yet, once upstairs, she was a different person – remarkably good on the bed, very enthusiastic. Even then, she very rarely spoke. Men would sometimes be slightly put out by her silence – but she was so good-looking that they overcame their embarrassment by the time the next party came around.

———— □ ————

# THE WATCHER • It takes all types to make a party swing and not everyone is necessarily going to want to join in the fun upstairs. Some of the quieter guests, particularly the women, prefer to sit back and watch the various entertainments on offer, whether it

be a striptease or a couple of the guests making an exhibition of themselves. After all, they're not the sort of thing most people are likely to see every day. Your duty as a hostess is to make everyone feel at home, whatever they happen to be doing, or watching, or a bit of both.

───────── ◻ ─────────

# THE GATECRASHER • Anyone who becomes known for holding good parties is going to have problems with people who turn up without being invited, and this is particularly difficult for the hostess holding a sex party. The last thing you need is a noisy confrontation on your front doorstep which could alert neighbours to what's going on.

I would always insist that my guests told me if they were planning to bring a friend so that there was never too much of a problem with gatecrashers. On a few occasions, a neighbour leapt the wall and joined in but he was a nice boy and put on a good exhibition, so I never objected.

───────── ◻ ─────────

# THE TRANSVESTITE • Apart from the Exhibitionist, there would be no one more welcome at my parties than the Transvestite. In my experience, transvestites are colourful, amusing, interesting people and, of course, they were always keen to come to my parties – after all, there's no one more interested in coming to a kinky experience than the average transvestite.

There's one thing that you as hostess should understand about transvestites. They tend to be very mean with money. At my parties, they'd be there free of charge, drinking my drink, having a lovely time, yet they never so much as brought a bottle. It took me a while to figure this out. When the transvestite takes on a woman's role, he wants it to be entirely convincing, right down to having everything paid for. They associate paying out with being a man – it breaks the spell.

There was one incident that brought this fact home to me. For years, I had been particu-

PARTY TYPES

THE TRANSVESTITE

PARTY TYPES

THE ACTIVIST

larly friendly with a transvestite, Michel. I had invited him to my parties, helped him come out, stood by him when he had the operation, been a friend to him when he was going through some difficult times. Then, for the first time in ten years, he managed to get off with a bloke – he and this little Indian went upstairs. Later on at the party, he came out to the kitchen and held a luncheon voucher out to me – in those days, the girls would get ten pounds when they handed in a luncheon voucher. And here was Michel, after all those year of help and free entertainment, demanding payment.

'Michel,' I said, 'Are you having a joke?' And he looked at me very seriously and said, 'No, Cynthia, I'm not.'

It was only the next day that I realized why he behaved like that. After all those years he had found someone who fancied him enough to pay him as a woman. Nothing, not even Madam Baloney, was going to take that away from him.

# THE ACTIVIST

'The sensitive hostess will discourage the discussion of religion or politics,' they say in the etiquette books. This has rarely been a problem at Ambleside Avenue, where the guests' chief concerns are more along the lines of 'Who am I going to go upstairs with?' 'When's the exhibition coming on?' or 'Will I have the time/energy to go upstairs a second time before the end of the party?'

In my view, people who are still thinking about politics when sex is on the menu are a bit of a pain, particularly when the party political broadcast continues both downstairs and upstairs as it did with an Indian girl who used to come to the parties. She was very beautiful and always in demand, but she had politics on the brain. A bloke would take her upstairs and, as soon as they were on the bed, she'd come like *Yesterday in Parliament*. This tended to be a bit off-putting – it wasn't what he was expecting at all.

In the end, I had to tell her, 'It's politics or sex in this house – not both. When you come to my parties, you leave your politics at the door.' But she couldn't stop herself from doing a spot of canvassing in the bedroom so eventually I stopped inviting her.

I'm all for a bit of bedroom activism – so long as it's of the traditional, non-verbal type. Keep politics out of sport, I say.

———— □ ————

# THE VIRGIN

I used to get all sorts at my parties but, on the whole, virgins – or at least men who admit to it – have been few and far between. Yet one of my most regular guests had been a virgin when I first met him –

a sixty-five-year-old virgin.

We had been in contact for some time by letter, ever since he first wrote to me through a contact magazine. He was in hospital at the time and I used to send him sexy pictures to cheer him up. When he came out of hospital, I met him and he explained that he had never had sex in his life – he had lived for many years with his mother who, on her deathbed, made him promise that he would never get married so that he could look after his mentally retarded sister. As you can imagine, he was a bit down, living his life without sex. You could see the sadness in his eyes.

Of course, he was nervous about coming to a party but, when eventually he did, he thoroughly enjoyed himself. It had been a long wait for him but, he said, it had been worth it.

———— □ ————

# THE SECURITY RISK

The greatest problem for the hostess who is entertaining in an adventurous and interesting way is that there is always a risk that one of your guests may for some reason decide to grass on you to the police or to a journalist. The reason may be to curry favour or to gain money, but the result is always the same: trouble. And, in my experience, it's always one of the girls that go bent on you.

There's no way of spotting the Security Risk beyond following your instincts about a person. There was one girl who always used to give me an uneasy feeling when she came to my parties. She had a hard mouth about her. She would sometimes look at one of my guests, an older man who was quite wealthy, and say, 'Ooh, I'm going to get him. He's all ready for me,' and normally she would. Yet she was popular with the men, very good on the bed, so I ignored my instinct and kept inviting her.

It turned out to be a serious mistake. She tipped off the press that I was holding the occasional party with some quite well-connected people putting on exhibitions, and soon I was back on the front page, 'CYNTHIA'S AT IT AGAIN'.

> THE HOSTESS OF AN EVENING PARTY MUST BE ENDOWED WITH A GOOD DEAL OF DIPLOMACY. ONE THING SHE MUST SET OUT TO DISCOVER IS: ARE THERE ANY OF MY GUESTS BURNING WITH A DESIRE TO DISPLAY SOME SPECIAL TALENT?
> *How to Make an Evening Go, 1925*

The Transvestite   The Gatecrasher   The Watcher   The Freeloader   The Undercover Policeman   The Security Risk   The Wallflower

The Exhibitionist     The Virgin          The Truant     The Snoop Journalist          The First-Timer     The Activist

# THE SNOOP JOURNALIST •

Although I get on very well with people from the press, I've never been very keen on the idea of my parties being infiltrated by journalists. Life's never the same after you've been a hot front-page story in the Sunday papers. One moment you're living a quiet life in suburbia, holding the occasional party, giving a few people a good time, the next you're on *The Joan Rivers Show* talking about the bank manager who liked mud being thrown at him. It's all very strange.

Fortunately, the Snoop Journalist who comes to a party, pretending to be a guest, is never too difficult to spot. He tends to be more interested in observing people than in getting any sex. He's always very interested in people's names and, in particular, what they do for a living.

The sure way to find out whether a guest is an intruder from Fleet Street or Wapping is to get a man friend at the party to mention quite casually that he can't be out too late tonight since there's an important debate at the House. If the guest shows any sign of unusual excitement, then you may well have a Snoop Journalist in your midst.

———— □ ————

# THE FREELOADER • In the early

days, I normally expected my guests to bring a bottle. It wasn't obligatory – 'You don't have to bring a bottle – my bottle's enough,' I used to say – but simply a way of saying 'Thank you'. After all, what other party could a man come to and know that he was virtually certain of finding a woman?

Yet, quite often, a man, in particular the

Then as now, certain party types are instantly recognizable.

43

PARTY TYPES

THE VIRGIN

PARTY TYPES

THE FREELOADER

stay too long because he had told the wife that he was just popping down to the pub. He'd spend a couple of hours at the party, go upstairs, have a sandwich and a lager, and then nip off back home with a real look of achievement on his face.

Sometimes I used to think that I must have been depriving the publicans of some of their best customers by the number of husbands who used the pub as an alibi to get to my parties.

□

THE ROWDY • It's a great mistake for a hostess to think that she needs the Jack-my-Lad type to make a party go with a swing. They tend to be all the same – boisterous, macho, and usually much more interested in being seen with a woman than in the sex itself.

In the early days, I used to invite quite a few younger men to my parties, but, after I moved to Ambleside Avenue, I decided that it just wasn't worth it. They used to make the older guests feel ill at ease with all their showing off and noise. I remember the incident that clinched it for me. We were all enjoying a party and everything was going well when one of the girls waiting in the queue on the stairs came down and told me that a couple of the younger men were misbehaving.

I stormed out of the lounge and there they were – sliding down the banisters.

'You can stop that right now,' I shouted, 'you're not doing that sort of thing in my new house.'

They looked quite surprised. They thought that anything went at Cynthia's parties, but that's where they were wrong.

Just because it was a sex party, there was no need for nice behaviour to go out of the window. They were never invited again.

□

THE UNDERCOVER POLICEMAN • Unlike most policemen, who are usually the hail-fellow-well-met types, the Undercover Policeman is more

Jack-my-Lad type, would come along without a bottle, drink my drink, eat my sandwiches, take one of my girls upstairs, all for nothing. He seemed to think that the pleasure of his company was enough.

If this happened several times, I might not invite him to the next party and the Freeloader would normally get the message. He was having too much of a good time to risk not being invited again.

□

THE TRUANT • The Truant comes to your party because it gives him the thrill of the forbidden. The greatest pleasure he gets is not from the sex itself but from the idea that he's put one over his wife, who thinks he's at work or down at the pub.

One of my regular guests was a very docile bloke in his fifties with a defeated, hen-pecked sort of look about him. He used to be a regular visitor at my evening parties but he could never

# THE UNDERCOVER POLICEMAN

## *Some Tell-Tale Signs*

■ He arrives with a burly friend in tight trousers and eye-shadow.

■ He stands to attention automatically when introduced to a guest who happens to be a senior police officer.

■ He disappears frequently to the bathroom to liaise with the boys outside with the help of a hidden walkie-talkie.

■ He wears regulation underpants under his frock.

■ He circulates the room, restlessly searching for someone to beat him.

■ He gooses one of the prettier french maids and suggests he might like to come upstairs.

■ He looks at his watch and straightens his clothes as if expecting a sudden, unexpected visit.

Down at the police station

On active sex party patrol

difficult to spot. I don't know whether they have a special course at Police Training College these days, 'How to infiltrate a sex party without being caught with your trousers down', or whether policemen are just more experienced, but the standard of Undercover Policemen seems to have improved over the years.

No hostess likes to feel that she's being infiltrated, so here are a few hints on spotting an Undercover Policeman.

## Conversation

The Undercover Policeman tends to conduct a conversation by asking a lot of questions. If one of your guests is showing a great interest in what everyone is up to, then be on your guard. If he's spotted in a corner making notes in a notebook, you should move quickly.

## Social Graces

Most people at a sex party are relaxed and happy. The Undercover Policeman has many reasons for being unhappy – he may be wishing he could go upstairs but is worried how it would look in court, he may be cursing that he's not out on a more straightforward job (like chasing burglars or riot control), he may be uncomfortable in his cocktail dress – and all these problems tend to make him a bit restless. He'll probably spend most of the party circulating among the guests, ears flapping, occasionally making the sort of suggestive remarks he thinks people at sex parties make.

## Dress

The more experienced Undercover Policeman will manage to blend in well with the other guests. During my last raid, one policeman came as a hearty Farmer Giles gentleman-farmer (and made a good job of it, too), the other came as a very unconvincing bisexual. In my experience, there's no truth in the rumour that some Undercover Policemen wear hobnail boots under their cocktail frocks.

## CHAPTER 8

# A GUIDED TOUR TO THE HOUSE OF 1,001 DELIGHTS

## THE HALL

*Naturally, where I receive guests needs to have a warm and welcoming feel to it on party day. It was here that, in the early days, I used to distribute luncheon vouchers.*

## THE GROUP SEX ROOM

*Except at Christmas, when it was opened up to all the guests, in the old days the downstairs Group Sex Room was used as a bedroom. It was called the Group Sex Room after we put two mattresses in there, allowing guests to double up, if convenient.*

— □ —

## THE CONSERVATORY

*Reserved for drinks and sandwiches, the Conservatory was normally out of bounds for couples wanting to get to know one another.*

## THE LIVING-ROOM

*I used to clear the centre of the room before parties so that there was enough space to circulate. The striptease would normally take place near the door.*

## THE BATHROOM

*In spite of all my efforts, couples would on occasions insist on jumping the queue by using the bathroom for purposes other than what it was meant for. This made them very unpopular with guests who needed it in the usual way.*

## THE GARDEN

*In summertime, drinks would be served on the lawn and guests would pair off to go inside when they felt like it.*

## MADAME'S BEDROOM

*Being a good hostess, I was always prepared to give up my own bedroom for the enjoyment of the guests. Of course, I made sure that my more valuable possessions were locked away first.*

□

## THE KITCHEN

*Because there was food around, I tried to discourage guests from misbehaving in the kitchen, although now and then brief exhibitions did spill over into the eating area.*

## THE STAIRCASE

*On occasions, the staircase was the busiest part of the house, with some couples queuing for the bedrooms upstairs, others coming down having finished upstairs.*

## THE MIRROR ROOM

*The most popular bedroom in the house, the Mirror Room was always in demand among guests who liked to see what they were doing. Sometimes a man at the front of the queue would be prepared to wait for it to become free, even though another room was available.*

*'No, you play through, old boy,' he'd say to the guest behind him, 'we're waiting for the Mirror Room.'*

## THE SHOE ROOM

*Knowing the importance of correct footwear for keeping your slaves happy, I need plenty of space for my extensive selection of high-heels.*

## THE PRINCESS ANNE ROOM

*Not named, as some guests might have hoped, after a distinguished royal visitor to Ambleside Avenue, but because it was the favourite room of a girl who, in her prime, looked the dead spit of Her Royal Highness. It was this room which the police entered so unceremoniously during the last raid. I'm still waiting for them to mend the door.*

## CHAPTER 9

# ENSURING THAT YOUR GUESTS GET ON

# ROMANCE AT A PARTY • The
fact is that, for the vast majority of people, the age of romance is dead. Ask any woman who's been approached by a young man at a party. You can forget the seductive chat, the compliments, the gentle cheek-to-cheek around the dance floor – all he's looking for is a lay, and he makes the fact pretty obvious.

On the other hand, the older man is very often thoughtful and romantic. He realizes that a woman can't just switch on and off like a light bulb. Oddly enough, it's when a woman reaches about forty that she becomes *less* romantic and more practical. That's why the age-mix at my parties – older men, younger women – used to work so well.

————— □ —————

# SOME NOTES ON THE
OLDER MAN • A lot of people have been surprised that I've always preferred entertaining men past their forties. These days we take youth very seriously and it's generally assumed that the best parties are those for the young.

I disagree. In my view, a man in his fiftes or sixties is, in many ways, at his prime. He's no longer the rowdy type, he's prepared to enjoy himself but not at the expense of others, he has come to terms with his own needs. He knows what he wants – and at my parties he used to get it.

Of course, my experience has mostly been with men who have been through the first flush of love and marriage and who are starting to get a bit restless. Perhaps the wife has lost interest in sex after she's had a couple of children, or simply the husband needs a change now and then, because, whatever people like to think, it's

not in a man's nature to be sexually devoted to one woman all his life. This was where I came in.

Older men used to come to my parties or, earlier, to the brothel and, although their wives may not have seen it this way, they both benefited. From the age of fifty or so, no man wants to put his family life at risk – he's too comfortable, he loves his kids – but he still needs his bit of fun.

Unlike a lot of women, most men will still be interested in sex into their sixties and seventies and, without it, they can become very depressed and moody. Often I see a group of older men sitting in a pub on a lovely day, drinking for hour after hour because there's nothing else to do. As soon as I walk in, I see their eyes light up.

'What d'you want to spend your life in here for?' I'll say. 'If my place was still open, you wouldn't be here, would you?' And they all have to agree.

Sex is a great rejuvenator. I've seen it with so many older men, including my father. If they have the chance to be with a young girl (and maybe they don't do much more than hold her or look at her body), it makes them feel young again. It's the best medicine a man can have in his old age.

I had never quite realized the hold that sex has on some men until I said goodbye to my dear Slave Rodney for the last time. He was very ill in hospital, unable to speak and hardly conscious. I was very upset to see him like that and I wanted to think of something to cheer him up during his last hours.

There was a television on in the background and, as I was standing there, I noticed that Gloria Hunniford's *Sunday, Sunday* show was on and that Gloria was wearing nice high-heels as usual.

'Slave Rodney,' I said firmly in my superior mistress voice, 'Look at the television. There's Gloria Hunniford and she's wearing lovely black stockings and patent leather high-heel shoes – your favourite.'

Very slowly, he turned his face towards

the televison and, although he didn't actually smile, I could see that silly expression that used to come over his face when I wore high-heels at home, and I knew that I had got through to him, with the help of Gloria Hunniford.

———————— □ ————————

# SELECTING A FEMALE PARTNER AT A PARTY •

Probably the best way for a man to find a suitable companion at a party is to keep an eye on what's happening on the dance floor. The experienced observer can tell a lot about a girl from the way she dances. The light, boyish types who move about a lot are almost certainly very active on the bed. If a girl is slinky and glides around the dance floor in a very seductive way, she's probably quite a sensitive, inventive sort of person when it comes to going upstairs.

But don't make the mistake of judging entirely by first impressions. Some of my best girl guests have been rather mousy and shy in normal social conversation but they soon lose their inhibitions in the bedroom. One of my oldest friends is a real lady downstairs, yet upstairs she's as wild as anyone I know. Appearances are important – but are not everything.

———————— □ ————————

# SELECTING A MALE PARTNER AT A PARTY •

Like a gallery owner can assess a picture, or a publisher can spot a bestseller, I'm good at men. I know what they'll be like sexually almost as soon as I meet them. After all, I've made quite a large study of the subject – for years I'd been interviewing a dozen or so men every day as a prostitute's maid, I've been a mother and, of course, a hostess. That sort of background gives you a good idea of how to sum up a man.

Unfortunately, this is a skill that can't really be communicated, since it's largely a question of instinct. But here are some general guidelines.

1 *The Shy Type* is usually a very quick, straight in-and-out character. At a party

many years ago, one of my more experienced girls found that her services were required upstairs by two separate guests who had approached her. 'I'll have the shy one first,' she told me in a very matter-of-fact way, 'he'll be all over in five minutes.' And she was absolutely right.

2 *The Jack-my-Lad* may take a lot of work upstairs. His greatest interest in the world is himself and, once there's no one around to whom he can show off, he may need a lot more reassurance than you might have expected.

3 *The Stout Party* will, for the obvious reason, tend to be passive, and he'll be looking for a woman more or less to make love to him. For myself, I find that very boring. In this respect, I'm quite conservative – I'm a great

53

THE SHY TYPE

THE MACHO MAN

believer in the missionary position. Some people who know me well are surprised by this – they seem to think I'm the dominant type and that I'd like to be in control. How wrong they are. Personally, I was never interested in being the boss in the bedroom.

4 *The Macho Man* is one of life's takers, not givers. He's only interested in himself, what he can get out of you and how quickly. He's always on the hurry-up – he's got to do this, he's got to have that, he's got to get back to

his wife. There was a time when I used to fall for this type but not any more. Now I'm more likely to be interested in the type who takes the time to understand me, downstairs and upstairs.

5 *The Quiet, Reserved Type* is often far better on the bed than the macho, in-and-out merchant. He may not say much when he's in company but once he's in the bedroom, he's more self-confident than anyone. Quiet and unassuming out of bed, dominating in bed – that's my ideal.

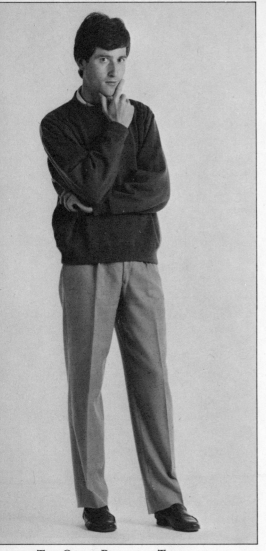

THE QUIET, RESERVED TYPE

THE JACK-MY-LAD

**IS THREE A CROWD?** • I've never found threesomes particularly interesting but there are some people who love them. I'll always remember meeting a group of very ordinary, middle-aged people – a married couple and a male friend – at the Organized Swing Party I once attended. They all looked as pleased as punch.

'Ooh, Cynthia,' said the wife, with a gleam in her eye, 'You'll never guess – we've just had a threesome.'

'Very nice,' I said.

None of them were anything to look at but it was clear that they had all enjoyed the experience. Thinking about it later, I could see there was something in it for all of them.

The husband was pleased that some other bloke fancied his wife.

The wife was pleased that, after years of being ignored by her husband, she could interest him and the other man.

The other man was pleased to be involved in anything kinky that happened to be going.

For me, there was something a bit sad

> THE YOUNG GIRL, THOUGH SHE
> WOULD BE DEFERENTIAL AND HELPFUL
> TO HER ELDERS, SHOULD NOT BE
> INSISTENT IN OFFERING ATTENTIONS.
>
> Lady Troubridge, *The Book of Etiquette*, 1926

about the whole thing but, who knows, perhaps it saved their marriage.

———— □ ————

# MAKING FRIENDS OVERNIGHT: TWO CASE STUDIES • As an experienced hostess of many years' standing, I'm often asked what makes some men successful with women while others, who may be just as good-looking and generally acceptable, are total flops. I'm normally tempted to answer: sheer nerve.

As the seduction techniques of two old party-going friends of mine prove, the gentle art of seduction is often only one short step away from the not-so-gentle art of deception.

## 1 *Barry from Heathrow*

Barry was a porter at Heathrow airport, not particularly good-looking but a crafty bloke, and nice with it. He was a tenant of mine for a while and I used to take a friendly interest in his sex life which, to start with, was frankly unexciting. 'Few and far between' would just about sum it up.

Then, suddenly, it all changed. Night after night he would bring back these charming and lovely girls who would stay the night in his room and then leave, never to be seen again.

It turned out that Barry had perfected an almost fail-safe seduction technique. Every evening at about midnight he would put on his uniform, newly pressed, and wander down to Victoria Station. There, almost without fail, he would find a girl who had missed the last train home. Now girls don't usually go off with strange men but somehow the uniform gave Barry a sort of authority, particularly when he told them he was an airline pilot.

So, although he had no money and not much personality, Barry used to bring these girls home to his scruffy room in Vauxhall. They used to be very appreciative and more often than not they would show their appreciation in the best possible way. And Barry, the 'airline pilot', would have lift-off.

## 2 *Snap-Happy John*

John used to come to some of the early parties but, after a while, he stopped bothering – he had so much crumpet in his everyday life that he had no need for sex parties.

He was a reasonably good-looking bloke, with a good line in patter, who used to get in touch with girls whose names he found in contact magazines by presenting himself as a professional photographer of models. It was the oldest trick in the book even then, but somehow the girls used to fall for it.

John would hire a room from me for the afternoon and would arrive with his model toting camera and tripod. Then it would be snap-snap, chat-chat, a bit of topless maybe, and, before long, all thoughts of photography had been forgotten. Of course, there was never any film in the camera and, if the girl happened to ask for prints, John was nowhere to be found. One afternoon per model was usually enough for him.

## CHAPTER 10

# SOME DIFFERENT
# TYPES OF PARTY

# THE BIRTHDAY PARTY •

Perhaps one of the most memorable parties of my life was for my son's sixteenth birthday. In many ways, it was the sort of party you would expect – cake, candles, lots of noise and laughter – but I like to think that the present I gave him made it a bit special.

Towards the end of the party, I gave him ten pounds and the address of a lovely girl who I knew would be good for him. A few weeks before, he had been to bed with someone else but, for various reasons, it was no more than a dry run for the real thing.

The girl was apparently quite surprised to see him on her doorstep. 'I don't usually go with young men,' she said.

My son kept quite calm. 'I'm Cynthia's son,' he said, 'and you're my birthday present.'

They had a laugh and were soon in bed together. In fact, it was such a successful birthday present that they went out together for a year after that.

So, in a way, I didn't give my son something for his birthday so much as take away something – his virginity. But I think he was grateful all the same.

———— □ ————

# THE SPANKING PARTY •

I've had some wild parties in my time but, without doubt, one of the strangest was the Spanking Party I once held at Ambleside Avenue.

My friend the Psychologist was behind it all. By nature, he was basically slavish but, because he was interested in the whole domination side of things, he once advertised himself as 'a master requiring a slave girl'. The first I heard of it was when he rang me to explain that he had found a slave girl. 'She's really nice but a bit nervous about the whole thing.' He wanted to know if I'd like to meet her. Of course, I was fascinated – I'd met no end of slave men in my time but never slave girls – so we arranged for him to bring her round to Ambleside Avenue one night at nine o'clock.

In the end, we spent a very interesting evening together. I was required to dress up in black and look very forbidding, the Psychologist was very good-looking and masterful in a suit, while this woman, who was forty-five, had two children, but had the figure of a twenty-one-year-old, acted out a naughty schoolgirl fantasy. I've never seen anything like it, before or since.

It was some time later that the Psychologist hit upon the idea of a Spanking Party. We invited eight or nine men and the Psychologist brought his slave girl. It was all quite low-key and good-humoured – nothing nasty at all – and she allowed three or four of the men to boss her around and give her a bit of spanking. To tell the truth, it's not something I'd particularly want to do again – there's not much else to do at a Spanking Party except spank – but it was certainly very different from any other party I've held.

In the end, the Psychologist lost patience with his slave girl. He didn't mind acting out a scene with her now and then but, with her, it was a twenty-four-hour job. When he took her out to dinner, she used to look at him and say, 'What I am allowed to eat, sir?' After a while, it started to get on his nerves and he stopped meeting her.

The last time I saw her was at a drag ball. She was in handcuffs and with a dog-lead around her neck, walking behind a mean-looking bloke with a crew-cut. At least she had moved on from being a naughty schoolgirl.

———— □ ————

# THE GARDEN PARTY •

There are definite advantages and disadvantages to holding your party in the garden. The advantage is that, when the weather's good, it can be really genteel and nice. A table with cucumber sandwiches, a couple of French maids bringing tea to the guests out on the lawn – what could be more civilized?

The problem is, when sex is available (and there's no such thing as a really successful party without sex), the security aspect can be difficult. A Dance of the Seven Veils on my back

lawn, for example, would soon have the neighbours leaning out of the windows to get a better view, and soon the whole thing could degenerate into a public spectacle.

It's a shame when you think about it, but I'm afraid that the sort of party I like best can really only be held behind closed doors.

———— □ ————

## THE FUNERAL PARTY •

There's nothing like a party for cheering people up, which is why I would never discourage anyone from turning a funeral, at a certain point, into a full-scale party.

This first occurred to me when I was burying Mitch, the Squadron Leader, back in 1981. We had come back to Ambleside Avenue from the church and everyone was sitting around in the lounge, looking very sober and respectable, talking in low voices about what a nice bloke Mitch was, what a laugh he'd been. Suddenly I thought, that's right – the last thing

Mitch would have wanted was for his friends to be sitting around getting depressed.

'That's the respectability bit over,' I shouted. 'Let fucking commence.'

And soon the party was in full swing. Quite a few of the girls were there and so were a lot of my regular men guests, and before long they were all trooping upstairs and having a lovely time. There were one or two of Mitch's friends who had never been to one of my parties – they were a little bit startled to see what was going on – but, apart from that, it really appealed to my sense of humour, Mitch's funeral turning into a sex party. I only wish he could have been there to enjoy it himself.

I'm not saying that all funeral parties should go this way, but the fact is that they can be depressing events. And in my book there's only one true cure for depression – sex!

———— □ ————

## ON BRINGING BLUE FILMS TO A FUNERAL PARTY: A POINT OF ETIQUETTE •

If holding a sex party after a funeral is impracticable (because it's being held in an elderly relative's house, for example), I'm greatly in favour of cheering people up in other ways. For instance, there could be a case for bringing along a few of your best blue films and a projector to the occasion.

I've shown a few blue films at funerals in my time and, on the whole, they've been quite popular. I showed one at my father's funeral but then my cousin objected so we had to stop it half-way through – it wasn't so much the lack of respect that she was worrying about as what the rest of the family would think.

So, choose your funeral carefully before bringing out the blue films. I refused to show them at Mitch's funeral party because his view had always been that he thought they degraded women. On another occasion, when my cousin's mother died, I brought some along with a projector, hoping she had changed her mind, but she still wouldn't have it. But, at the right funeral, blue films can go down a treat.

## ON SELECTING THE RIGHT BLUE FILM FOR THE OCCASION • *Casanova and the Nuns* is a good one – very sexy and quite funny too. Unfortunately, every time I get hold of a copy, I'm raided. The police must like *Casanova* too, because I've never got it back from them.

———————— ◻ ————————

## THE NUDIST PARTY • Nudism is very popular in some parts of Europe and I suppose that no book on home entertainment would be complete without a word of advice about nudist parties. I've only experienced one party where all the guests were nude from beginning to end, as opposed to stripping off on a part-time basis, and I have to say it was one of the most boring evenings of my life.

It was during a holiday I was spending with Mitch at a nudist holiday camp in Yugoslavia. At first, I was very reluctant to strip – I had just had my kidney operation and I was

> THE MAN OR WOMAN WHO DOES NOT
> PLAY GAMES MISSES ONE OF THE
> KEENEST PLEASURES OF LIFE.
> Rose Henniker Heaton, *The Perfect Hostess*, 1931

rather worried about how my tummy looked. Mitch reassured me, saying that I had a lovely back, legs and breasts, that every woman had something beautiful about her, and that I was probably one of the most attractive women there. Eventually, I stripped. I went shopping stark naked, wearing only a pair of sun-glasses to hide my embarrassment. Of course, Mitch was right to force me to go out in the nude. I was as unashamed as anybody after I had walked around starkers for a couple of hours.

The problem with a Nudist Party is that there's no sex about because everybody's so used to seeing each other without any clothes on. In fact, the party at the nudist camp was one of the most respectable I've ever been to. Most of the guests were couples, with a lot of German and Austrian bank-manager types. The nearest thing to a party game was a volley ball competition and, frankly, seeing a load of middle-aged women with their breasts bobbing up and down as they chased after the ball was hardly my idea of a good time. The problem was that wearing no clothes all the time took the mystery out of sex and, without the mystery, what's left?

So, my word of advice on nudist parties would be: don't.

———————— ◻ ————————

## THE LEATHER PARTY • I've never been that interested in the sort of party where everyone is waltzing about in tight leather skin suits and metal bracelets, although I know they're very popular in some quarters. Of course, it can be quite amusing to watch men with collars round their necks being led around the room. Personally, I prefer my slaves to do something useful, like clean up the house.

Occasionally, some of the girl guests at my parties have arrived in leather gear, and very nice they've looked too. At my most recent trial, the prosecution decided that anyone wearing leather was interested in sado-masochism. Unfortunately for their case, the Duchess of York had recently been photographed in a leather skirt.

'If it's good enough for Fergie,' I said, 'it's good enough for me.'

———————— ◻ ————————

## THE ORGANIZED SWING PARTY • One of my great regrets is that, because I'm so well known for giving parties myself, people tend not to invite me to theirs – I think they worry that anything they do could never quite compare with mine. 'Oh, our parties are a bit mundane,' they'd say, 'you wouldn't be interested.' It used to annoy me because I love parties, even straight ones – in fact, it would have made a change from all that sex.

I've only been the guest at one social event where sex was definitely on the menu – and, without wishing to sound prudish, it quite put me off. I found it almost distasteful.

The party was organized by a sex magazine for guests that they called 'swingers'. It was all very discreet, with the venue being kept secret until the very last minute. I had been invited by the man who ran the magazine and, although it meant staying overnight at a hotel in Birmingham, I agreed to go, out of curiosity more than anything else.

What a disappointment it turned out to be. Despite it being summertime, it was pouring with rain when we all gathered in this large, draughty barn next to a caravan site in the countryside near Birmingham. The guests were mostly middle-aged swingers and wife-swapping couples in their late fifties and they were all determined to have a great time.

My host's wife was a prim little woman who obviously disapproved of the whole thing and, after a while, I found that I was half agreeing with her. After people had eaten and drunk, there was an odd sort of show – three or four middle-aged women jumping about in suspender belts and kinky stockings – and then they started pairing off for the main business of the party. Some of them went into the caravan site, others actually did it behind a screen in the barn itself. It was all very odd.

I was sitting with my host's wife watching all this coming and going and it was quite clear that she wasn't enjoying herself at all.

'Here,' I said, 'Where's the hot running water and French letters and disinfectant?'

She called her husband over and asked him the same question, but in a very sarcastic tone of voice.

'Oh, they don't need that,' he said, looking a bit uneasy.

I thought even then how sad it was that ridiculous parties like this have to happen, all so hush-hush and on the quiet. How much nicer it would be if we had fun houses in Great Britain, where people could enjoy themselves at their leisure by the fire and in nice surroundings, rather than cavorting about and degrading themselves in a barn.

'These parties are not like yours were,'

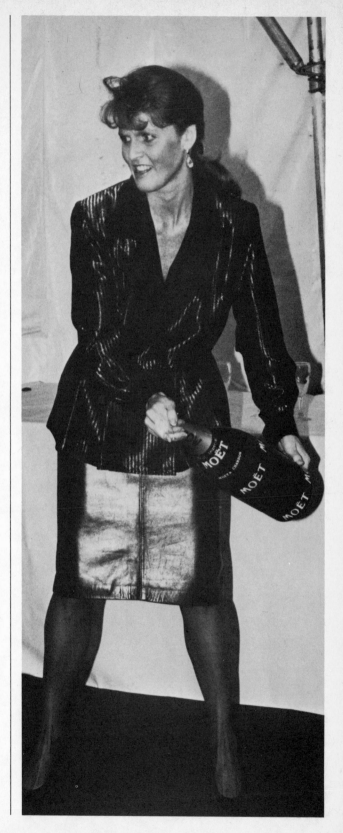

said one man who happened to recognize me. 'They had to pay at yours – this is all free.'

Quite right, I thought, and most of the men I know would prefer to pay out a few quid than end up at a party like this.

———— □ ————

# THE APPLIANCE PARTY •

There is no doubt that women are at their most uninhibited if there are no men around. When it's all girls together, you see a side to the female character that would surprise a lot of men.

I was once invited to a party where sexy gear was being sold to a group of housewives in Streatham. It was all a bit low-key for me but still very interesting. I felt I understood women a bit better after hearing them talk and laugh about sex, their husbands and boyfriends.

I even invested in one of the appliances myself. A dear writer friend of mine was always intersted in the female breast – so I bought him a mug in the shape of a tit. I hope he didn't take it personally.

———— □ ————

# THE CANDY CLUB PARTY •

If there was ever a party which showed me how ridiculous the sex laws in Britain are, it was my trip to the Candy Club in Amsterdam.

It was during my brothel-keeping days and a man friend and I were taking a brief holiday in Amsterdam. More out of curiosity than anything else, we decided to visit the Candy Club, which had quite a notorious reputation at the time. When we arrived there, I thought we had made a mistake – it looked a real dive from the outside, with big, shabby steel doors. But, once they let you in, it was very different.

Although it was a sex club, it was not in the slightest bit seedy. Couples danced topless, girls in suspender belts, some men were down to their briefs, which personally appealed to me because men dancing stark naked were never much to my taste. Now and then, a couple decided to make love and other people would look on with a sort of friendly interest. It was

quite romantic in its way.

I think that there was a bit of showing off going on. My friend and I looked rather respectable and we kept all our clothes on, so they probably wanted to shock us. Little did they know that it was a bit of a busman's holiday for me, home from home, except that in England we would have been raided.

———— □ ————

# THE ROMAN ORGY • I experi-

enced my first Roman Orgy while staying in a hotel in Hamburg with my old friend Copper Henry in 1969. The Orgy Room was like something out of *I, Claudius*. It was decorated

all in white, with soft blue lighting, grapevines cascading down the walls and mattresses covering the whole floor. In the middle of the room, sitting around on soft cushions, were the other guests, all in togas like us – charming, easy-going people with whom I immediately felt comfortable.

Konrad brought in the food – pheasant, duck, chicken, all cooked in the Roman way – while we all chatted as if we were at a normal dinner party. By the end of the meal, I had clocked this old boy of about sixty, who was with a very attractive blonde. 'He'll do,' I was thinking, 'I'll feel easy with him.' But his girlfriend made it pretty clear that she wasn't

about to let him go. I began to wonder who on earth I was going to pick.

Now it wasn't so much to please myself as to please Copper Henry because, until I chose, he couldn't make a move either. At last I had an idea. I went to see Konrad at the bar. I was dead nervous because even during my Great Portland Street days I'd never chatted a bloke up for myself.

'Of course,' he said. 'It would be an honour.'

'I'll need romantic music in the background.'

He laughed and said he'd arrange it. By now, the idea was beginning to appeal to me. He

A lot of parties I go to these days are full of celebrities and people you read about in the gossip columns.

said, 'How about you and I starting the whole thing off?' And, almost to my own amazement, I agreed.

Which was how I came to give the one and only exhibition of my life. I think Konrad and I put on a good show. Certainly, everybody was very appreciative, particularly Copper Henry, who couldn't believe that I was behaving in such an outrageous fashion. I can't say it was the most exciting experience of my life – it's difficult concentrating with all those people looking on. I must have been nervous because apparently I was chatting away throughout the entire performance.

In fact, the moment I remember most clearly was when Konrad paused in the middle of the exhibition and said loudly in his strong Dutch accent, 'Woman, don't talk – do!'

———————— ▫ ————————

THE SHOWBIZ PARTY • A lot of the parties I go to these days are just full of celebrities and people you read about in the gossip columns. Much as I like the glamour and the excitement, I must admit I've been surprised by the number of false people I've met, compared to the world I used to know. At my parties, we knew what we were there for – the girls knew they were going to make money, the men knew they were going to get sex – there was no bullshitting about.

The world of film premières and celebrity parties is nothing like that. The people aren't nearly so genuine. It's all hustle, it's all on the hurry-up, and nobody seems to enjoy what they're doing. In fact, it's a good thing I've run a brothel for twenty years – I know how to weigh people up as soon as I meet them. Otherwise I'd have been exploited no end.

CHAPTER 11

# WHEN THINGS GO WRONG

# THE GUEST WHO COMES TOO EARLY

The problem with being known for giving good parties is that your guests are so keen to get going that they often arrive on your doorstep half an hour before the off. I'd be rushing around organizing things right up to the last minute and it threw me completely if people arrived early which, in my view, is more impolite than arriving late.

So, instead of being greeted by my usual warm smile, they used to be on the receiving end of a right bollocking. They normally only did it once.

□

# THE GUEST WHO COMES TOO LATE

On the other hand, it was very rare at my parties for the men to arrive late. They'd be there on the dot, anxious to get every minute of the party crammed in.

The girls were generally much less punctual. If it was an afternoon party starting at two, they would sometimes arrive at about three o'clock. It used to worry me because the nightmare of any hostess is that she has an unscheduled stag party on her hands. They always turned up in the end, but there were some tricky moments.

□

# THE GUEST WHO ONLY WANTS ONE THING

In the early days, I used to get the occasional bloke who would arrive, go upstairs, pay me and leave – all before the party had really got going. My advice to partygivers is to discourage this kind of guest – if you can't enter the spirit of the thing and spend the whole afternoon or evening enjoying yourself in company, what's the point of it all? Luckily, most of my men stayed for the whole party – in fact, the problem was getting rid of them when it was all over.

□

# THE GUEST WHO CAN'T HOLD HIS DRINK

One of the most important pieces of advice I could ever give a party-giver is: never ever invite someone who you know really likes to drink. Your party can be going really well and then suddenly the bloke that's been knocking it back starts getting sleepy or sloppy or even downright aggressive. That can kill a party stone-dead.

Of course, the newcomer at a sex party may be a bit shy and, in that case, I'll turn a blind eye to their needing an extra drink, particularly if it's a girl who doesn't know me and is nervous. So I would tend to forgive them on the first time they got a bit tipsy. But if I could see a girl or one of the guests was a drinker, I'd never invite them back.

□

# HANDLING A MAN WHO HAS HAD ONE TOO MANY

However hard you try, you'll always have the occasional bit of bother with someone who has drunk a bit too much. Now and then, at a normal party, a bloke might become aggressive but, in my experience, this happens very rarely at a party where sex is on the menu.

The fact is that, if a man is going to have sex, he's as sweet as a lamb. As any policeman will tell you, half the arguments and Saturday-night fights that take place are over women – there are ten or fifteen blokes competing for maybe five or six girls. Now, if you supply a party where the men know that women are going to be available, there's no reason to be aggressive.

The other secret of a peaceful, friendly party lies in the age of your guests. For example, I was catering for men over forty – their fighting days were over. They had other things on their minds. But, put a number of young men together at a party and you could have trouble.

On those very rare occasions when I've noticed that a man looks as if he's had a few drinks and could get aggressive, I had a simple solution – female charm. I'd just get one of the girls over to him, to talk to him, put her arm round him, reassure him about whatever was worrying him. It's a trick I learnt in prison. I used to watch the officers calming down the girls who were upset by just talking to them through the slot in the door, listening to their problems, spending a bit of time with them. Almost always, the girl had been causing trouble because she was worried about something or was feeling lonely and she simply wanted someone to take notice of her.

Very often, it's the same with men who have flown into a temper about something. It's not the drink so much as some other problem coming to the surface – and there's nothing like a good girl, spending time with him, to calm him down.

————— ◻ —————

# HANDLING A GIRL WHO HAS HAD ONE TOO MANY • For some reason, it doesn't work the other way round. If a girl gets drunk and a man comes up and puts his arm around her, she'll probably get worse. I've only had one experience of a girl drinking much too much and, if I hadn't known what to do, it could have ruined the whole party.

She was a lovely girl, blonde, and, I was told, very good in bed. But, at one party, this Italian gentleman came up to me, rather upset, and said that he had just been upstairs with this girl and that she had been very unpleasant and aggressive towards him. I was surprised at first but when I saw her, all flushed and unsteady, I could immediately see what the problem was.

It took very careful handling. If I took her side, the Italian would have been annoyed; and if I blamed her, she probably would have rushed out of the house screaming and cursing, upsetting the neighbours and causing all sorts of trouble.

So, although I was angry and I thought the girl had done wrong, I didn't show it. I gave the Italian his money back and paid her myself, trying to keep her calm by flattering her a bit and soothing her because I could see that she had a scared look in her eyes. I suggested she call a taxi from the house and, as she was dialling the number, I kept talking to her, stroking

her hair and telling her how nice she looked. Eventually she went off quiet as a mouse and the crisis was over.

So my advice to any hostess faced with a spot of the drunk and disorderly problem is to keep calm, use flattery – and never invite them back!

————— ◻ —————

# MISUSE OF THE BATHROOM • When a party's going very well, especially upstairs, there's always the danger of an overspill from the bedroom causing problems in other parts of the house.

I had a particular problem with the bathroom – as well as queues for the bedroom,

people would be waiting outside the bathroom because there would be a couple in there using it in a way bathrooms weren't meant for.

It got so bad that I had to place a sign on the door, which was duly photographed by the police when they raided me. What they found so interesting in a little notice, I'll never understand.

> THE BATHROOM IS A PLEASANT PLACE
> BUT PEOPLE MAKE IT A DISGRACE
> I HARDLY LIKE TO TELL YOU
> THE HORRID THINGS THAT PEOPLE DO.
> Evelyn St Leger, 1931

# NEIGHBOURS: A SEVEN-POINT PLAN

HOWEVER understanding your neighbours may be – and I've been very lucky as far as Ambleside Avenue is concerned – it won't be long before they start taking an interest in your parties, particularly if sex is very much on the menu. It only takes a few incidents which are out of the ordinary in your area – scantily dressed guests in the back garden, French maids with hairy legs, the occasional police raid – for the net curtains to be twitching all down the street.

There are certain basic rules concerning neighbours which should be followed at all times. Depart from any of these guidelines and you could find yourself in trouble.

## 1 Discourage your lady guests from advertising your party as they arrive

When I first used to hold sex parties, one or two of the girls used to turn up on the doorstep dressed to kill, all made up, wearing a sexy low-cut dress – at 2.30 in the afternoon. I used to go barmy.

'Get in here quick,' I used to say, and they would ask me what was wrong. I'd have to explain to them that, if you're coming to a day-time sex party, it's not exactly sensible to come tripping down the street in high-heels with your boobs half hanging out. Suspicions tend to be aroused. At all costs, encourage your lady guests to arrive in an old coat and scarf – they can get themselves dolled up once they're inside.

## 2 Insist your French maids keep their city suits on until the party starts

Again, it's simply good sense for French maids to arrive straight and wait until the door is closed behind them before they get 'in character'. Luckily, most of my transvestites have been most discreet and, apart from the occasions when they've been bundled off to the police station in cocktail dresses and suspenders after a raid, the neighbours have been spared the sight of them out of the closet.

## 3 Use a side door whenever possible

The moment of greatest danger as far as neighbours are concerned is when your guests are arriving one after another, ringing the bell, and generally hanging around on the front doorstep. If you have a side door that can be left open, people can get in quickly, quietly and without encouraging the curiosity of the neighbours.

## 4 If you live in a flat, make sure your guests know the right number

One of the great mysteries of the male sex is that, while a man has no difficulty in remembering something like a girl's measurements, memorizing the number of a flat is often beyond them. 40-26-38, that they can manage: Flat 11 at Number 15, and you can bet your life they'll call Flat 15 at Number 11.

That was finally how I lost the place in Great Portland Street, where I ran 'a business consultancy' as Judith Mansell. Men would ring me, I'd give them the address and strict instructions not to call after 7.30 at night, and a few days later they would turn up after midnight and at the wrong address. Now this can happen a few times and the neighbours will ignore it but, if the door happens to be opened by an attractive young girl and the first question from the businessman on her doorstep is, 'Do you give a personal service?', then you've got problems.

## 5 Avoid warning your neighbours in advance that a party is to take place

Because my parties were quiet affairs – there

## How To Make Your Entrance

INCORRECT

CORRECT

were some wild goings-on but we were never noisy about it – I never saw the need to warn the neighbours that I was entertaining, particularly if we were going to use the garden. Word would quickly get around, since my house is over-looked by several others, and in no time we'd be performing for an audience of most of the neighbourhood!

### 6 Always be prepared to extend a warm welcome to your neighbours

There may be some neighbours who aren't the slightest bit disapproving of your parties. In fact, what they want most of all is to be invited. This is normally to be encouraged.

For instance, many years ago a former neighbour of mine, a good-looking, young, married bloke, soon wised up to the sort of parties I was holding and used to hop over the fence whenever his wife was out and I was entertaining. At first I was a bit put out – after

all, I'd never invited him – but he was such good company, slipping out of his clothes almost as soon as he arrived, and sometimes putting on a bit of an exhibition with one of the girls, that I never objected.

My attitude was always that as long as your neighbour was prepared to contribute to a party, to put something in as it were, he was wel-come.

### 7 Be discriminating when it comes to inviting neighbours in

On the other hand, neighbours can bring trouble with them. Back in Great Portland Street, the wife of one of my men, a charming Indian gentleman, became suspicious about the visits her husband paid. It was through her front window that the police set up an observa-tion post and finally ended my seven happy years there. So, neighbours need to be treated with care.

## RESPONDING TO UNWELCOME CORRESPONDENCE FROM WIVES • Naturally, not many wives know about the sort of parties I used to hold and, if they did, most of them turned a blind eye to them. I should think they realized that my parties did their men a power of good.

But, as a hostess, you must be prepared to receive the occasional letter from a wife who doesn't appreciate what you're doing. My policy is not to reply, unless it's really necessary but, if it is, to do it quickly and politely.

For instance, I once received a letter on cheap lined paper during the days when I was running the brothel in Great Portland Street.

'My husband can't even afford to buy me clothes, let alone come and visit you,' she wrote. 'In fact most of my clothes I have to buy in jum-

ble sales.' It was quite a short letter – not nasty, not friendly, but almost begging. It finished, 'Please don't see my husband again if he comes visiting.'

I felt so sorry for this woman that I wrote back to her in quite a sympathetic way. Unfortunately, as I explained to her, there were so many men who used to call me, I had no idea who her husband was, or even if I knew him. I never heard from her again.

## THE DANGER OF BEING MISUNDERSTOOD BY UNINVITED GUESTS • If you think that your party might be the subject of interest from the local constabulary, make sure that any notices you put up around the house are not

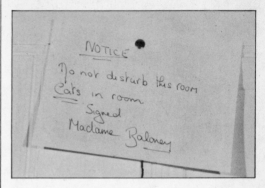

open to misinterpretation. This innocent notice, for instance, was once photographed as evidence against me. Fortunately, my cats were not called as witnesses.

———— □ ————

## ON BEING RAIDED BY GANGSTERS • It was some nine months after I'd moved into Ambleside Avenue when I discovered that somehow news of my parties had fallen into the wrong hands.

It was about three o'clock on a party day and everything was going perfectly. All the men were in the living-room enjoying the entertainment, a Dance of the Seven Veils by a stripper called Helen. Then, just as she had got down to her last two veils, the bell rang.

Now, normally I wouldn't answer the door at this time – I used to say if the men don't get here by two o'clock, it's too bad – but on this occasion I did. A rather strange-looking man stood on the doorstep.

'I'm sorry,' I said, 'you can't come in.' Too late – three men burst in. They were carrying guns.

At first, when they went into the living-room wearing face masks, people thought it was part of the act. But then, when the guests realized what was going on, all hell broke loose. Two of the gangsters rounded up the men in the living-room but they must have been useless at the job because soon men were escaping through side doors and girls were climbing through windows. Helen, the dancer, managed to get away, but she was in a fright and dashed half-starkers out into the street. She ended up hiding in the neighbours' bushes.

'You'd better hurry up and go,' I said to the gangster, 'I've got a policeman upstairs in the bedroom.'

Well, that did it. The gangsters decided to cut their losses. Within seven minutes of breaking in, they were off, sprinting across the road. Of course, this terrified Helen in her two veils, who was convinced that they were chasing her. So she dashed screaming around the back of a house, breaking a pane of glass, and hammered on the door of an old man in a bedsitter at the back. You can imagine what a pleasant surprise that was for him – one moment he's sitting there watching televison on a Sunday afternoon, the next he's being invaded by a twenty-six-year-old dancer without any knickers.

———— □ ————

## ON BEING VISITED BY COPPERS ON THE TRAIL OF GANGSTERS • Some
ten or fifteen minutes later, a patrol car turned up and from out of the window I could see two youngish coppers carting Helen, still half-

naked and hysterical, across the road to the house.

To tell the truth, I was a bit annoyed at her for panicking but I was determined not to show it in front of the coppers because that would be the sort of thing they would be looking out for. So, when they came in and the girl kept saying, 'I'm sorry, Cyndy,' I was just as casual and friendly as I could be.

'Come in, Helen,' I said, 'I'm awfully sorry. Are you all right?'

The two coppers were looking at me very suspiciously but really I was a picture of respectability, all dressed up in black. 'Thank you so much for bringing her in,' I said, putting on a big smile.

'So what's up here then?' said one of the coppers.

'Well, I was just giving a small afternoon party,' I said, and could see by the way my guests looked that that was how it appeared to be.

They asked about the men with guns.

'That was just a toy gun,' I said. 'It was

one of the girls' boyfriend who was a bit jealous of her coming to a party without him. It was just a joke.'

One of them picked up a couple of French letters that were on the bedside table.

'Some party,' he says, with a big, cheeky grin on his face. 'Come on, Mrs Payne, I'm broad-minded.'

'Yeah,' I said a bit more firmly, 'I'm broad-minded too.'

So, a bit reluctantly, the coppers took a few more statements from the guests and the girls.

'What went on in here?' one of them asked a guest in the living-room. 'Blue films?'

'Oh, no, officer. Better than that.'

'I see,' said the policeman, assuming it was a joke.

By now, we were acting very casually and the policemen had begun to see that they weren't going to get anything here.

'We may be back,' one of them said as they were leaving.

'Oh, yes, please do,' I said, 'Any time you want.'

Nine months later, we were raided again, only this time it wasn't villains with guns. It was the boys in blue.

## CHAPTER 12

# REMAINING ON GOOD TERMS WITH YOUR LOCAL CONSTABULARY

## NEVER TAKE A POLICEMAN FOR GRANTED

• I've been out with policemen, helped them with their inquiries, fallen in love with them, been raided by them, been to bed with them, been to court with them – work or play (or somewhere in between), I reckon the British copper and I know each other pretty well. And, although I've had my difficulties with the Law over the years and I disagree with them frequently about the kind of prosecutions that they bring, I still believe we have the finest police force in the world. As far as I'm concerned, there's no country in the world where I'd rather be raided.

Yet the fact is that, for whatever reason, coppers do like to take the closest interest in activities which some people insist on believing are harmful, like sex. For this reason, no hostess can afford to take her local constabulary for granted. She should know as much as possible about dealing with the average policeman, including – most important of all – how to behave during a police raid.

———— □ ————

## THE ART OF DISCRETION

• To be honest, there are few people less well qualified than I am to talk about keeping a low profile as far as the Law is concerned. Dur-

ing my career, I've been raided eight times. The first six were during the days when I had a flat in the West End and were relatively civilized affairs. Two or three policemen would barge in waving warrants. 'We have reason to believe this is a brothel blah-blah,' and so on. 'What are you talking about?' I'd say, knowing the game was up. They'd look in the bedrooms and find a couple of girls entertaining men, and it was off down to the station. All very straightforward.

By comparison, the last two raids were like World War III. Vanloads of policemen screeching to a halt outside the door, thirty or forty policeman bursting through the front door, gentlemen at play interrupted by coppers who didn't even bother to knock, bedroom doors reduced to firewood, a major traffic hold-up on Ambleside Avenue as yet more police vehicles, including an interview coach, arrived, sackloads of harmless material (letters, party photos, shopping lists, magazines) confiscated for months, police photographers snapping away at every inch of the house from the kitchen to the lavatory (with particular attention being paid to the bedrooms), the whole place being turned upside down in a desperate hunt for lewd material, the cats being thoroughly disturbed – all for a blinking party. It was a strange business.

I've never quite understood why police have taken such an interest in me. The first six visits I could understand – if a neighbour complains about there being a brothel next door, they have to act – but the reason for the major raids has always been a mystery to me.

Certainly, I've tried to be as discreet as possible, and I've failed. I hope that the sensible hostess reading this book will learn from my experience.

———— □ ————

## ON RUBBING A POLICEMAN UP THE WRONG

WAY • I've usually been pretty honest in my dealings with the police because I recognize that, like me, they have a job to do. This attitude, the respect of one professional for

Breaking and entering: A member of the local constabulary helps me with my enquiries in what's left of the Princess Anne Room following the 1987 raid.

another, has helped me considerably over the years. I've never had a copper ask me for money and frankly it would horrify me if I heard that a policeman was taking bribes. If it did happen, I probably wouldn't grass on them – but I would tell them where to put it, even if it meant risking more trouble.

———— □ ————

# ON RUBBING A POLICE-MAN UP THE RIGHT WAY
• On the other hand, I've heard that quite a lot of this goes on, particularly in the Shepherd's Market area. So my advice to the hostess meeting a policeman who urgently wishes to take down her particulars in the course of his investigations is to tell him to move along there and sharpish – or words to that effect.

———— □ ————

# THE PRIVATE LIFE OF THE POLICEMAN
• In the event of an unscheduled interruption of your party by two or three dozen policemen from the local cop shop or the Vice Squad, it's useful for the hostess to know a little about your visitors. So here, based on a lifetime of close, first hand experience, is a candid guide to the inner workings of the average policeman.

**1** *He is extrovert and fun-loving.*
From the early days, I've always enjoyed mixing socially with coppers because normally they are very good company, of the macho, hail-fellow-well-met type. If you want your party to go with a swing, you could do a lot worse than invite a few policemen who know how to relax when off-duty.

**2** *He can be rather mean.*
Like all Jack-my-Lad types, the party-going copper tends to think that his presence is enough at any party. Many's the time in the past when I've had to bawl and shout at a copper who's arrived for a party, grinning all over his silly face, without even a bottle.

'Where's the blinking whisky or brandy?' I'd say, and he would be rather apologetic and promise to bring one next time.

**3** *He is often very attractive.*
As many women will agree, there's something about a policeman. Whether it's his authority, or uniform, or simply that the force attracts good-looking men, I wouldn't like to say. During a period of fifteen years, I had three boyfriends who were coppers, all of whom I met socially. In fact, I was with one of them, on and off, for seven years and I was very much in love with him, but, what with him being married and a copper, it became a bit complicated.

**4** *He is sexually confident.*
The fact is that coppers get plenty of opportunities in their line of work and, after a while, many of them develop a sort of ease with women, a confidence, which adds to their attractiveness.

**5** *He may be a disappointment upstairs.*
The policeman has a lot more aggravation in his work than most men do. Combine that pressure with the fact that they have to do a lot of socializing in pubs to get their information (and, of course, drink and sex don't go together at all), and you can end up with a man who has serious problems in his private life. In fact, most policemen I've met have difficulty getting it up, and are quite prepared to admit that it's the job that causes the problem. Personally, I think it's rather sad, particularly when you think of the important work they do.

> FOR PARTIES WHERE YOU MUST HAVE ONE EYE ON SECURITY, FOR INSTANCE IF MEMBERS OF THE ROYAL FAMILY, PROMINENT POLITICIANS OR CELEBRITIES…ARE EXPECTED, MAKE SURE THERE IS ONLY ONE ENTRANCE TO THE PARTY.
> *Lady Elizabeth Anson's Party Planners' Book,* 1986

## CHAPTER 13

# RAID ETIQUETTE
## FOR
# POLICEMEN

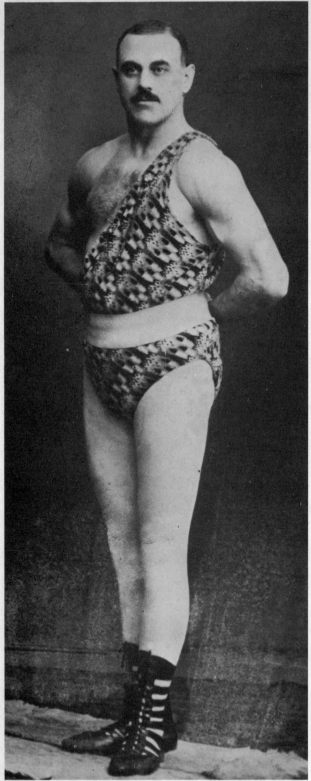

If you must infiltrate a party, make sure your cover is well thought-out and plausible.

# PLANTING YOUR UNDERCOVER POLICEMEN • If you must infiltrate a party, make sure that your cover is well thought out and plausible. The policemen planted for my last party were a good example of the rights and wrongs of disguise.

'Peter Tollington', also known as Police Constable Stuart Taylor, masqueraded as a fifty-year-old gentleman-farmer who had lived in Egypt for some years and now lived with his sister-in-law. He was unmarried and lonely. Although, looking back on it, his green tweed suit was a little obvious and his beard had plainly been dyed grey, he was generally plausible as a new guest.

His brother-in-law, 'Harold', a bisexual played by Police Constable Jack Jones, was altogether less convincing. His green eye make-up was way over the top, his tight trousers didn't fit and the old-fashioned spectacles he wore on the end of a gold chain were frankly eccentric. If anything, he looked more like the dummy in *Educating Archie* than a guest at a Cynthia Payne party.

□

# GETTING YOUR STORY RIGHT • While the gentleman-farmer's reasons for being at my party were quite convincing, Harold was once again a disaster. He claimed to be a bisexual but, by poncing about in eye make-up and a floppy silk shirt, he should by rights have blown his cover immediately. Clearly no one had told him that bisexuals do not as a general rule wear make-up. If Harold had presented himself as an honest-to-goodness transvestite, he would have been altogether more plausible.

□

# DO NOT BE CHEAP • When Peter Tollington arrived in full Farmer Giles gear for his first party, he took the trouble to behave correctly. He kindly presented me with a bunch of roses and a box of chocolates, and kissed me gallantly on the hand. As a result, I took an immediate liking to him.

By the time he arrived for his second party, this time with Harold in tow, his standards were slipping. There was no present, not even a bottle, and no kiss on the hand. I suppose I should have guessed he was a copper there and then. A less generous hostess would have complained and it was only because I don't like to disappoint guests that they were able to come in and co-ordinate the raid they had been working on for so many months.

— □ —

# INVITING YOUR COLLEAGUES IN BY MEANS OF A SIGNALLING DEVICE •

Peter Tollington, the gentleman-farmer, was most thoughtful when it came to setting the raid in motion. He locked himself in the bathroom and, by means of some sort of transmitter hidden about his person, gave the message to proceed to his colleagues down the road. He then told me he needed to get something from the

car. I opened the door – and the next thing I knew the hall was full of policemen. It wasn't really necessary, since I would have let them in anyway, but it certainly reduced the risk of my front door being taken off its hinges like it was last time.

> HEARTS, LIKE DOORS, OPEN WITH EASE
> TO VERY, VERY LITTLE KEYS
> AND DON'T FORGET THAT TWO OF THESE
> ARE 'YES, I THANK YOU' AND 'YES, PLEASE'.
> Rose Henniker Heaton, *The Perfect Hostess*, 1931

# AVOID SURPRISING GUESTS AT PLAY EXCEPT WHEN STRICTLY NECESSARY •

I know that there's not much room for politeness and decorum during a police raid, but a certain degree of tact will be much appreciated by the older partygoers.

A certain degree of tact will be much appreciated.

For example, one of my guests was said to be sitting on the side of the bath, relaxing with a friend (in contravention of 'house rules'), when a couple of police constables burst in without so much as a by-your-leave. The girl was naturally startled and leapt to her feet with an appropriate expletive, in the process knocking my guest over backwards into the bath.

Such scenes are embarrassing for all concerned and best avoided.

——————— □ ———————

# ALLOW GUESTS TIME TO FINISH WHAT THEY ARE DOING BEFORE INTERVIEWING THEM • At an earlier party,

two policemen burst into the Mirror Room to find an elderly gentleman on the bed with a girl, and at a most important part of his performance.

'We are police officers,' they said, 'Stop what you are doing.' The old boy hardly missed a stroke.

'I don't care who you are,' he said. 'I'm not stopping now.'

I always thought it was very generous of the two policemen, who were quickly joined by a policewoman, to allow the bloke to finish, although perhaps it would have been more tactful to wait outside the door, rather than to gather round the bed, making unnecessary comments.

CHAPTER 14

# THE
# PARTY'S
# OVER

THERE'S nothing in life quite like a really good party on a glorious English summer's day. Outside on the lawn, people are relaxing over a cup of tea served by a willing French maid. Pretty girls are chatting animatedly to old friends. Upstairs, behind closed doors, guests are enjoying themselves as only they know how. On the landing at the top of the stairs, a couple are putting on an exhibition for those waiting for the bedrooms.

What better way could there be of spending an afternoon?

I still can't believe that the law of the land forbids me to hold any more of my traditional parties. These days I'm often a guest at film pre-mières and book launches and, looking around at the characters I see on these occasions – producers, starlets, publishers, PR girls – I can't help feeling that these occasions have more to do with money and contacts than my parties ever had. We all prostitute ourselves in one way or another. The only difference between a showbiz gathering in the West End and an afternoon party at Ambleside Avenue is that mine were a darn sight more honest.

But I've done all my shocking now. Over the years, I've enjoyed shaking people up, shocking them out of their little square boxes. I've done all the outrageous things I want to do and, looking back on it all, I can see I've won through. These days, there's no one left to shock.

I'll probably go on giving the odd party, now and then. I can't help myself. I might even give one to help this book along its way. Of course, it won't be like the old parties. This will be a quiet, civilized, decorous, well-ordered, downstairs affair.

I think.

> TO BE A GOOD HOUSEWIFE DOES NOT NECESSARILY IMPLY AN ABANDONMENT OF PROPER PLEASURES OR AMUSING RECREATIONS.
>
> *Mrs Beeton's Book of Household Management*, 1861

The party's over.

# APPENDIX

# MY FANTASY PARTY

One day I'd like to hold a party which brings together old friends from the past with some of the celebrities in whose circle I find myself moving these days. All the food and drink would be organized by an outside caterer, allowing me to circulate among my guests, ensuring that they are having a good time. Of course, there would have to be an exhibition – though perhaps a really good striptease would be more suitable for the occasion – and then, when all the guests were relaxed, they would be free to go upstairs with their chosen partner if the mood took them.

## THE GUEST LIST FOR MY FANTASY PARTY WOULD DEFINITELY INCLUDE:

Jim 'Nick Nick' Davidson

Slave Philip

Tom Jones

Ken Livingstone

Viscount Weymouth

Paul Bailey, my author

Bernard Bresslaw

'Dirty Dai' Llewellyn

The Masochist Bank Manager

Bernie Winters

The Doctor

Quentin Crisp

Boy George

Su Pollard

Mary Whitehouse

Samantha Fox

Janet Street-Porter

The Indian Princess

Agatha

Barbara Windsor

Princess Anne (of the Princess Anne Room)

Fergie

Jenne Casarotto, my agent

The Doctor's Girlfriend

Julie Walters

Boy George's Mum

Kenneth Grant, my solicitor

Chief Constable James Anderton

Judge Brian Prior, Q.C.

David Leland, my scriptwriter

A French maid

Barry Humphries

Alf Dubs

The Psychologist

Les Dawson

Chief Inspector Colin White of the Obscene Publications Squad

Mandy Rice-Davies

Cleo 'Knockers' Rocos

Rabbi Julia Neuberger

Marilyn Warnick, my publisher

Dr Ruth

Dame Edna Everidge

Angie Best

The Psychologist's Naughty Schoolgirl Slave

Princess Michael of Kent

Cynthia Payne

# HAVE YOU GOT WHAT I

*Anyone can hold a straightforward, run-of-the-mill party, but entertaining at home in a truly interesting, upstairs-downstairs style takes practice and ingenuity.*

*Answer the questions in this quiz to discover whether you have the very special qualities required of the modern hostess.*

DO YOU SEND OUT YOUR INVITATIONS ON:
- [ ] A Embossed invitation cards?
- [ ] B The back of slightly saucy postcards?
- [ ] C Discreet but sexy plain paper?

AS YOUR STRIPTEASE ARTISTE ENTERS THE FINAL STAGES OF THE DANCE OF THE SEVEN VEILS, YOUR MOTHER ARRIVES ON A SURPRISE VISIT. DO YOU:
- [ ] A Burst into tears and beg her forgiveness?
- [ ] B Pretend that you're holding a fashion show?
- [ ] C Give her a rollicking for turning up late?

WHAT IS MOST IMPORTANT TO YOU AS A HOSTESS?
- [ ] A Laying your party plans correctly?
- [ ] B Laying your table setting correctly?
- [ ] C Laying your guests correctly?

YOU DISCOVER THAT AT LEAST FIVE OF YOUR GUESTS ARE UNDERCOVER JOURNALISTS. DO YOU:
- [ ] A Throw a mackintosh over your head and run out of the house, screaming, 'No comment!'?
- [ ] B Send out for more drink?
- [ ] C Hold an impromptu auction for exclusive publication rights to the inside story of the party?

AS YOUR GUESTS POSE FOR A PARTY PHOTOGRAPH, DO YOU TELL THEM TO SAY:
- [ ] A 'Cheese'?
- [ ] B 'Moneeee'?
- [ ] C 'Lesbian'?

# ʼAKES TO BE A HOSTESS?

YOU NOTICE THAT ONE OF YOUR GUESTS HAS A WALKIE-TALKIE STUFFED DOWN THE FRONT OF HIS TROUSERS. DO YOU:

- ☐ A Spill chilli sauce all over it?
- ☐ B Warn the other guests to behave themselves?
- ☐ C Crouch down and shout into it, 'Come on in, boys – we need more men!'?

EDWINA CURRIE MAKES A SURPRISE VISIT TO YOUR PARTY ON A FACT-FINDING MISSION FROM THE MINISTRY OF HEALTH. DO YOU:

- ☐ A Lock yourself in the toilet?
- ☐ B Discuss the merits of muesli over bangers and mash?
- ☐ C Explain that she has to wait in the queue for the Mirror Room just like anyone else?

A HUSBAND AND WIFE MEET UNEXPECTEDLY AT YOUR PARTY. DO YOU:

- ☐ A Lock them in the kitchen to sort it out between themselves?
- ☐ B Tell her that personally you think he looks really nice in her best cocktail dress?
- ☐ C Introduce them as if they were strangers and hope they go upstairs together?

WHAT IN YOUR VIEW IS THE BEST SIGN OF A SUCCESSFUL PARTY?

- ☐ A Receiving a number of nice 'Thank you' letters the day after the party?
- ☐ B Being obliged to use threats and a cattle-prod to remove the guests from the premises?
- ☐ C Discovering as you clear up the next day a bra hanging from a curtain rail, leather underwear in the rose bushes and a naked tax inspector asleep in the bath?

## HOW DID YOU SCORE?

### MOSTLY A's
*You have a long way to go. Start quietly with the occasional tupperware party before embarking on the big time.*

### MOSTLY B's
*You show distinct promise but need to improve a bit before your parties can become really disreputable and fun.*

### MOSTLY C's
*Please send me an invitation as soon as you plan your next party.*

# ACKNOWLEDGEMENTS

EDITOR: Terence Blacker

DESIGN: Alex Evans and Paul Elms at Shape of Things

PHOTOGRAPHY: Mike Prior, assisted by John Slater

ILLUSTRATION: Colin Hadley (chapter openings), David Stoten and Tim Watts (pages 40, 41, 44), Phil Chidlow (pages 24, 25)

PASTE UP: Clive Frampton

PICTURE RESEARCH: Sara Driver

MODELS: Wentworth Dillon (French maid on the cover and throughout the book), Elisha Scott (Cover), Terry Sachs (page 45), Dessi Murphy (pages 54, 55), Peter Gates Fleming (page 75)

ADDITIONAL PHOTOGRAPHY: John Londie (page 75)

ARCHIVE PHOTOGRAPHS: BBC Hulton Picture Library (pages 3, 43, 63, 70), Mary Evans Picture Library (pages 7, 12, 15, 22, 34, 59, 71, 86), Mansell Collection (page 8), Aquarius Literary Agency (pages 9, 14, 23, 32, 37, 79, 86, 87), Topham Picture Library (pages 22, 72, 78), Syndication International (page 53), Rex Features (pages 61, 64, 85), Press Association (page 85), Universal Picture Press (page 85), City Syndication (page 85), London Express News Agency (page 85). All other material supplied by Cynthia Payne.